Surveying the South

Surveying the South

Studies in Regional Sociology

John Shelton Reed

University of Missouri Press

Columbia and London

Copyright © 1993 by

The Curators of the University of Missouri

University of Missouri Press, Columbia, Missouri 65201

Printed and bound in the United States of America

All rights reserved

5   4   3   2   1   97   96   95   94   93

Library of Congress Cataloging-in-Publication Data

Reed, John Shelton.

   Surveying the South : studies in regional sociology /
  John Shelton Reed.

     p. cm.

   Includes bibliographical references and index.

   ISBN 0-8262-0914-9 (cloth).—ISBN 0-8262-0915-7 (paper)

   1. Southern States—Social conditions.   I. Title.

HN79.A13R393   1993

306'.0975—dc20   93-8561

                                             CIP

∞™ This paper meets the requirements of the
American National Standard for Permanence of Paper
for Printed Library Materials, Z39.48, 1984.

Designer: Kristie Lee
Typesetter: Connell-Zeko Type & Graphics
Printer and Binder: Thomson-Shore, Inc.
Typeface: Leawood

To the memory of friends:

Guy B. Johnson (1901–1991)

Edgar T. Thompson (1900–1989)

Rupert B. Vance (1899–1975)

Contents

A region is what its people make it and can be no better than the people who live in it. We, and you, and the people down the road, and the people next door, and the people in the next town, and the people in the next state—we are all the South. The South as a region is the sum of its parts, and we are the parts.

—*Exploring the South* (1949)

Preface

Fifty years ago, "regional sociology" was a flourishing enterprise, centered on Howard W. Odum and his students at the University of North Carolina. Its glory days were in the 1930s and 1940s, but it could be said to have finally expired not long before I joined the sociology department at North Carolina in 1969. Rupert Vance and Guy Johnson had come to Chapel Hill (from Arkansas and Texas, respectively) as students in the 1920s and had stayed on to make their careers there. By the 1960s, they were the last of Odum's many distinguished disciples still at work in anything resembling his tradition. Just as I arrived, fresh out of a Yankee graduate school with a brand new dissertation on Southern cultural distinctiveness, both men retired.

Although I jumped at the chance to teach Johnson's course on race relations and Vance's "Regional Sociology of the South" (I still teach the latter), that happy coincidence was not enough to put me in the apostolic succession: the brand of sociology I was trained in was too far removed from what Odum and his students professed for that. Still, I did get to know both Vance and Johnson, and also their friend Edgar Thompson, recently retired from Duke University, just down the road. (Thompson, a proud South Carolinian, had studied with Robert Park at Chicago and gone on to become probably the world's leading authority on the plantation as an institution.) These older men were extraordinarily gracious to a young colleague with distressing gaps in his knowledge both of the South itself and of the history of sociological work on it. Their patient tutelage instructed me in this splendid tradition and, in time, even allowed me to feel a part of it. If this volume's subtitle is an act of presumption, its dedication acknowledges a debt still outstanding.

In the years since 1969 most of my work has had to do, one way or another, with the South or, more precisely, with Southerners. (As the introductory textbook from which I have taken my epigraph suggests, for sociological purposes a region *is* the people who make it up.) The essays and articles collected here appeared originally in places ranging from *Science* to the *Virginia Quarterly Review,* but all have in common that they either exemplify or examine the study of the South—usually sociological, if not "regional sociology" proper.

The first three essays, for example, discuss the lives and work of some of the many Southerners who wrote about their region between the two world wars: Odum, regional sociology's founder and moving spirit; Vance, arguably his most accomplished student; and the Vanderbilt Agrarians, authors of *I'll Take My Stand,* men often seen, with reason, as the regionalists' great antagonists in the conflict between tradition and progress. The sketches of Odum's and Vance's careers (one presented to the Southern Sociological Society to mark the fiftieth anniversary of Odum's magisterial *Southern Regions of the United States;* the other originally the introduction to a collection of Vance's papers that Daniel Singal and I edited) are relatively conventional, if admiring, summaries. "For Dixieland," on the other hand, is both an attempt to situate Agrarianism as a social movement and something of an exercise in the sociology of knowledge. (It was written for a Vanderbilt symposium on the fiftieth anniversary of the Agrarian manifesto, naturally a celebratory and primarily literary affair.)

The next three chapters are essentially follow-ups of earlier studies. "The Incredible Shrinking South" looks at how the boundaries of the South and of "Dixie" (not quite the same thing) changed in the fifteen years after a mapping expedition in the early 1970s. Like the earlier study, it maps these regions by looking at the use of the words *Southern* and *Dixie* in the names of commercial enterprises. "Lazy No More" examines continuity and changes in regional stereotypes during roughly the same period. Within the limitations of its measurement and sample, it reveals a great deal of continuity and a few suggestive changes. Both chapters capitalize on the fact that the 1970s and 1980s were an eventful period for the South, which might reasonably be expected to have produced some changes (and also on the fact that I have been at this long enough now to begin to replicate my earlier studies).

"Too Good to Be False" had its start some time ago, when I published an article on lynching and was asked by the editor of the journal to refer to the (irrelevant) correlation between lynching rates and cotton prices because "everyone knows" about that. Looking into it, I discovered not only that many people did know about it, but that it wasn't exactly so. Two graduate students and I later chased down a great many references to this alleged fact and wrote this account of its curious history. (Because the point is not to embarrass individuals but to illustrate how science sometimes slips up, I have not named the researchers and textbook writers who serve as our bad examples; however, anyone who really wants to know can refer to the original publication.)

An East Tennessean may be more likely than someone from the Deep South to doubt that race is "the central theme of Southern history" (in Ulrich Phillips's famous phrase), but no one who knows the South can question its historical and continuing importance. Over the years, I have given more attention to what unites Southerners than to what divides them and more to aspects of the South that have not changed than to those that have; consequently, it is fair to say that I have not given race the attention it would obviously deserve in a comprehensive account of Southern life and culture. Nevertheless, the next three essays do address the subject.

"Birthrate *Brown*-Out" was written after my friend Ronald Rindfuss, a distinguished demographer, asked me one day in all innocence what had happened in the South in the spring of 1954 that could explain a subsequent decline in white birthrates. (At least I remember it that way. Ron denies it.) When I suggested the obvious answer, he went off to do some more computer runs and came back to report that the hypothesis had survived. The resulting article, with its bemusing conclusion, was published in *Science,* to what I felt to be a sort of embarrassed silence on all sides.

The other two essays examine changes in Southern race relations during and since the 1960s. "Jim Crow, R.I.P." was written for a magazine published by the U.S. Commission on Civil Rights at a time when it seemed (to me, at least: my co-author Merle Black can speak for himself) that it was becoming fashionable to minimize the accomplishments of the civil rights movement of the 1960s. It argues that the destruction of de jure segregation and of the white Southern public opinion that supported it was a remarkable piece of what can only be described as social engineering. In "Up from Segregation," which began as one of three Lamar Lectures at Georgia Wesleyan University, I argue that Southern race relations are now no worse than anyone else's and try not to sound smug about it.

Finally, the concluding chapter, "On Narrative and Sociology," was a presidential address to the Southern Sociological Society. Unaccustomed as I am to giving presidential addresses, when it came time to write this one I took the empirical approach, looking at what presidents had done in the past, only to find ample precedent for nearly anything. So I chose to do what is hard to get away with in any other setting, at least with any expectation of people's sitting still for it, and talked about some things I think sociologists should be doing differently, and about how sociology could be improved. This is not a subject of compelling interest to most nonsociologists, but I have included this homily here partly because what it urges may be applicable, mutatis mutandis, to other disciplines. Mostly, however, I have included it because it pays tribute to the tradition of Howard Odum and the other regional sociologists.

Acknowledgments

My most obvious debt is to my coauthors, as indicated under the titles of the essays that we wrote together. I have been privileged to work with such talented and agreeable colleagues. In addition, I thank Vanderbilt University, Georgia Wesleyan University, and the Southern Sociological Society for inviting lectures and addresses that eventually turned into several of the essays and articles reprinted here. For the small survey reported in "Too Good to Be False," I gratefully acknowledge the cooperation of the Society for the Psychological Study of Social Issues and the support of the Smith Fund at the University of North Carolina at Chapel Hill.

Two of these essays were written while I was a fellow of the National Humanities Center (supported by National Endowment for the Humanities grant FC-2038-81), and I worked on preparing this collection for publication as a fellow of the Center for Advanced Study in the Behavioral Sciences (supported by National Science Foundation grant #BNS-8700864). Once again, I thank the directors and staffs of those two splendid institutions for their invaluable support. Mike Crane and Alecia Holland at the Institute for Research in Social Science helped me with scanning documents and securing permissions, respectively, and I am grateful to them. I put the finishing touches on this volume while enjoying the true Southern hospitality of Millsaps College as visiting Eudora Welty Professor of Southern Studies. Everyone I dealt with at Millsaps was gracious and helpful, but I especially want to thank Robert King and Suzanne Marrs.

This being my third book with the University of Missouri Press and my fourth with its director, Beverly Jarrett, I hope it is obvious that I take great pleasure from that association. I thank Beverly, Jane Lago, Polly Law, and all the others at the press—those I know and those I don't—who have helped with this and the earlier books.

Dale Volberg Reed is still my best editor and critic, though. I thank her last, but not by a long shot least.

For permission to reprint copyrighted material, I acknowledge:

American Association for the Advancement of Science:

"Birthrate *Brown*-Out": originally Ronald Rindfuss, Craig St. John, and John Shelton Reed, "A Fertility Reaction to a Historical Event: Southern White Birthrates and the 1954 Desegregation Ruling," *Science* 201 (July 14, 1978): 178–80.

Hemisphere Publishing Corporation:

"Howard Odum and Regional Sociology," *Sociological Spectrum* 10 (April–June 1990): 155–68.

"Lazy No More: Changing Regional Stereotypes": originally "Continuity and Change in the Regional Stereotypes of Southern College Students, 1970–1987," *Sociological Spectrum* 11 (October–December 1991): 369–77.

Louisiana State University Press:

"For Dixieland: The Sectionalism of *I'll Take My Stand*," reprinted by permission of Louisiana State University Press from *A Band of Prophets: The Nashville Agrarians after Fifty Years,* edited by William C. Havard and Walter Sullivan. Copyright © 1982 by Louisiana State University Press.

University of North Carolina Press:

"Rupert B. Vance: An Appreciation," reprinted from *Regionalism and the South: Selected Papers of Rupert Vance,* edited by John Shelton Reed and Daniel Joseph Singal. Copyright © 1982 by University of North Carolina Press.

"The Incredible Shrinking South": originally "The Shrinking South and the Dissolution of Dixie," *Social Forces* 69 (September 1990): 221–33.

"On Narrative and Sociology," *Social Forces* 68 (September 1989): 1–14.

University of Texas Press:
"Too Good to Be False: Social-Science Folklore": originally "Too Good to Be False: An Essay in the Folklore of Social Science," *Sociological Inquiry* 57 (Winter 1987): 1–11.

Virginia Quarterly Review:
"Up from Segregation," *Virginia Quarterly Review* 60 (Summer 1984): 377–93.

"Jim Crow, R.I.P." was originally published as "How Southerners Gave Up Jim Crow," in *New Perspectives* (a publication of the U.S. Commission on Civil Rights) 17.4 (Fall 1985): 15–19.

Antecedents

Howard Odum and Regional Sociology

Howard Odum and his colleagues have received a great deal of attention recently. Sometimes, in fact, it seems that an entire generation of Southern intellectual historians is making careers of writing about the regionalists, who are often seen as part of the remarkable flowering of Southern talent between the world wars, best known for what it produced in literature and journalism. What could I possibly add to what Daniel Joseph Singal, Michael O'Brien, Morton Sosna, Wayne Brazil, and other historians have already said about regionalism? Still, if I did not discuss this subject, I do not know that any sociologist would. I have no particularly original thoughts about the regionalists, but at least I have given them *some* thought, which seems to be an unusual thing for a sociologist to do these days.

Sociologists like to quote Alfred North Whitehead's cruel maxim that a science that hesitates to forget its founders is lost, and for whatever good it does us it is certainly true that sociology in the United States has now largely forgotten the regionalists. Canadians seem to have better memories, perhaps because regionalism is a hotter political topic for them: Ralph Matthews, for example, treats them respectfully and at length in his book, *The Creation of Regional Dependency.* But in a 1973 study by Frank Westie, nearly half of a sample of new American Ph.D.s in sociology confessed without shame that they had never heard of the former president of the American Sociological Association. Another third said Odum's name was familiar, but they did not know his work. I doubt that the figures have changed for the better since then, so maybe one reason to discuss Odum and his colleagues is simply to honor these prophets a bit in their own country. I am happy to contribute what I can.

I am going to concentrate on Odum himself, for two reasons. In the first place, it was he, with Katherine Jocher, whose reputation and identity were most firmly linked to regional sociology, the discipline, and to regionalism, the associated ideology of regional planning and "balance." It is significant, I think, that regional sociology barely survived Odum. In fact, some would say it did not.

In the second place, as Guy and Guion Johnson demonstrated in their history of the Institute for Research in Social Science, it is almost impossible to generalize about the other regionalists. "Howard Odum's boys" (as they called themselves) and his girls (as they did not) were far from a homogeneous group. Odum was the school's founder, guru, and undisputed leader; to his credit, however, he was not out simply to clone himself. He gathered around him and nurtured a variety of men and women who did many different kinds of regional sociology and many different things in addition to regional sociology, and it is hard to say where one sort of activity stopped and another began.

Rupert Vance, my own favorite, was recognizably a modern social scientist, as much a demographer and human ecologist as a "regionalist." Especially toward the end of his career, he did regional sociology only on the side, as it were. Guy Johnson was as much an anthropologist and ethnomusicologist as a sociologist of any sort; a great deal of the work he did on race relations and black culture was less regional sociology, the study *of* the South, than studies simply *in* the South (to borrow a useful distinction from Edgar Thompson). Harriet Herring's work on industrial communities (much of the best of it, alas, never published) wears very well altogether apart from its regional, and regionalist, context. Half a dozen other scholars of stature who passed through Odum's orbit were regionalists for a time—maybe part-time—and moved on to other things.

As I said, this variety does not lend itself readily to generalization, so I am going to concentrate on Odum himself. At least what he did indisputably was regional sociology, if only because he said it was.

And it is hard enough to generalize about Odum. As the historian George Tindall wrote, in a sympathetic appreciation published shortly after Odum's death, he was "a man of unusual vitality, active not only as a creative scholar in his own right but as an organizer and administrator of scholarship and, what is more, persistently active in many aspects of public affairs."

Guy Johnson told me once about the time a black road gang was working on Columbia Street in Chapel Hill, near the present site of the Carolina Inn. Someone who knew of Odum's interest in black folk music rushed to tell him that the workers were singing as they worked. Odum scurried over from the Alumni Building, pad and pencil in hand, and perched on a wall to listen. He was scribbling away, getting the lyrics down, when he suddenly realized the workers were singing about *him*:

> White man sitting on the wall.
> He don't do no work at all.

But of course Odum was working right then, in his fashion. In that sense he was always working.

Odum's public life involved service on innumerable boards and commissions and councils devoted to the South and its problems. I will not dwell on that aspect of his career, although it was this work, more than his writings, that led the *Washington Post* to eulogize him in 1954 as "the Eli Whitney of the Modern South." Only Franklin D. Roosevelt, the *Post* wrote, might have had a greater influence on the South's development.

As an administrator, Odum bequeathed to Chapel Hill its Departments of Sociology, of Anthropology, and of Recreation Administration, its School of Social Work, its Institute for Research in Social Science, its Center for Urban and Regional Studies, and the journal *Social Forces*. I will just note that that legacy is still very much with us, although some of it in forms Odum would not recognize.

I will not linger over Odum's activities as a prize-winning cattle breeder, either. I will only report that I have heard that more than one North Carolina cattleman was surprised to learn that Odum was also a college professor.

I do want to talk a bit about Odum's scholarship, but even that is not easy to generalize about. As Tindall put it, Odum was "the victim of an active mind that raced on from one thing to another. . . . Consequently, he wrote more perhaps than he should have, and published practically all of it." Odum was so prolific for so long that examples can be found to contradict almost any generalization. Still, I will try to discuss a few noteworthy features of his prodigious output.

One generalization that will stand is that the unifying theme of all of his activities, including his scholarship, was service. In Odum's mind, at least, it all hung together. Even the cattle breeding was a matter of practicing what he preached, not only as a demonstration but also as a contribution of bloodstock to his program of diversification for Southern agriculture. The point of Odum's work—the point of his life—was to speed the day when more Southerners could work sitting on the wall; when fewer would be doomed to hard, hot, sweaty, monotonous, poorly paid labor on the roads, in the fields, or in the mills. Odum's gradualist, reformist program was very much a matter of working within the system, and people will no doubt continue to disagree about its effectiveness. But no fair-minded observer can doubt his sincerity or his dedication.

For better or for worse, Odum saw no contradiction, no disjunction even, between his scholarship and his political agenda. The title of the Johnsons' history, *Research in Service to Society,* pretty much sums up the story of Odum's work and of regional sociology in general. Gunnar Myrdal did not approve of much about the South, but he did like Southern social scientists. In *An American Dilemma,* he compared them favorably to their Northern colleagues because, he said, "statesmanship enters more naturally into [their] writings." Odum was a fine example of what Russell Jacoby has labeled the "public intellectual." Jacoby sees the type as an endangered species on American campuses, but if Myrdal can be believed, that seems to have been true even in the 1940s.

Much of Odum's scholarly reputation in his own time, and even more of what remains of it today, rests on his "scientific" writing, especially his empirical, policy-oriented research. But to my mind his most interesting work is some dreamy, impressionistic, historico-ethnographic—well, adjectives fail me, but Odum himself called the work "portraiture." The "Black Ulysses" trilogy (*Rainbow Round My Shoulder, Wings on My Feet,* and *Cold Blue Moon*), based on the recollections of a semimythical black vagabond; *An American Epoch; The Way of the South:* these books are seldom read now, and that is a pity.

In these works, Odum wanted to do justice to the complexity, the particularity of what he saw, to *get it all down.* Like the statistical compendiums I will mention in a minute, these books hose the reader down with a torrent of detail. Daniel Singal has observed that Odum's characteristic device was not the statistical table but the list, and he quotes Odum's amazing instructions to the artist who was drawing a map of the South for the endpapers of *An American Epoch.* Odum asked the artist to include:

> Monticello;
> colonial homes in east Carolina, Charleston, Georgia, Montgomery, Natchez, and "somewhere in Louisiana";
> farmhouses and Negro cabins "here and there";
> mill villages—at least one in Virginia, North Carolina, South Carolina, and Georgia;
> chimney stacks and factories, Muscle Shoals and other electrical works;
> cotton and cattle farms in east Carolina, Georgia, Mississippi, Alabama, "etc., and don't forget the mules";
> some "handsome" farms;
> resorts along the coast starting in Virginia;
> "fruit and flowers in the tropical part";
> coal in Birmingham and oil in Texas;
> skyscrapers to mark the major cities;
> a figure of Robert E. Lee on horseback;
> robed Klansmen, ditto;
> highways, with curves and hills in the mountains and overhanging Spanish moss on the coast;
> major ports marked by ships, "indicating commerce and exports";
> and "the old-time Negro and the new Negro as a unit" (whatever that means).

All this on a two-page map! And, perhaps to indicate that he did not pretend to have it all, Odum concluded: "If it could be done, I believe I should border the whole thing with question marks."

These books of Odum's are very much of their time and place. If suspicion of generalization is a Southern characteristic, they are certainly very Southern. In other ways, they are of a piece with such contemporary works as Stephen Vincent Benet's poetry or the novels of Chapel Hill's own Thomas Wolfe. Odum's accomplishment in these books and the sensibility they reveal are more literary than scientific, and they show us a man who is more interesting, and I think more sympathetic, than his works of sociological theory and research suggest.

Let me say a word about those theoretical works. Among the minority of sociologists who have any conception of Odum at all, a common misconception is that his sociology was, in the dismissive phrase, "merely descriptive." I would argue, in the first place, that there is nothing "mere" about description, done well. (I will come back to this.) In the second place, it is simply not true that Odum was not concerned with theory. His explication of "folk-regional theory" made up a substantial part of his work, by weight at least, and a conspicuous part, too, including his 1930 presidential address to the American Sociological Society. But this theoretical work has sunk into an oblivion even more profound than the rest of Odum's work. Why is that?

Even at the time, I should point out, it was not terribly influential. Indeed, I find little evidence that anyone outside the circle of Odum's colleagues and students paid much attention to it. In part, no doubt, this reflected the obscurity of the prose in which it was couched. But why should this have been a fatal flaw for Odum when it was not for, say, Talcott Parsons?

Frankly, I do not think folk-regional theory was very good theory, but that, too, is not always an impediment to success in our field. And, anyway, at least one scholar's contrary opinion deserves great respect: one of Rupert Vance's last published works was a 1972 *Social Forces* article that tried to rescue one of Odum's concepts from what Vance thought was undeserved neglect.

Some intellectual historian needs to take a look at Odum's central, organizing concept of the "folk." I suspect one could trace connections between Odum's thought and that of scholars like the folklorist B. A. Botkin and the poet Donald Davidson (one of the Vanderbilt

Agrarians who was, ironically, one of Odum's most outspoken academic adversaries), and show that Odum's way of seeing the world was not unusual for a provincial American of the 1930s. But for an American sociologist it was unusual—idiosyncratic and (worse) old-fashioned. "Folkish" thought, even without the unpleasant overtones it acquired after the rise of National Socialism, was not something that many of Odum's sociological contemporaries thrilled to. Their America was a pluralistic urban society—and Herbert Gans had not yet discovered his "urban villagers."

In other words, Odum's theory had little to do with what was going on elsewhere in sociology at the time. It looks to me as if Odum's theoretical efforts owed a great deal to his teacher Franklin Giddings and to William Graham Sumner, but I am out of my depth here. In its organicist assumptions, though, Odum's theory was certainly less like that of the Chicago School, or that of Emile Durkheim, or Max Weber, or even Talcott Parsons, than like—well, like that of Henry Hughes and George Fitzhugh, the two Southern proslavery theorists who introduced the word *sociology* to America in the 1850s.

Anyway, it is just not accurate to say that Odum's work, considered as a whole, was atheoretical. But it is fair to observe that Odum's theory had little to do with his students' research activities, or even with his own—and it is hard to see how it could have.

The curious fact is that, insofar as Odum's place in history rests on his writings at all, it rests on his policy-oriented, descriptive research. In that old graduate-school distinction, Odum tried to be nomothetic—Lord knows he tried—but his most influential work is his most idiographic. In plain English: this theory-ridden sociologist is best known for his least theoretical work. And rightly so, in my opinion.

Despite all his theorizing, Odum's typical research method was to shovel on statistics by the wheelbarrowful, pretending to let the facts speak for themselves and implying that readers could draw their own conclusions. Consider, for example, Odum's magnum opus *Southern Regions of the United States;* anyone who knows Odum only through that book probably thinks of him as a dry-as-dust fact gatherer. And, in fact, Odum sometimes liked to present himself that way, a practitioner of what we might call "Dragnet" social research ("Just the facts, ma'am.").

I do not know how disingenuous this was, and I am certainly not accusing Odum of bad faith. Nevertheless, this pose—and that is what it was—had useful consequences. It established Odum's credentials as a dispassionate, objective *scientist.* When he turned from describing the South's problems to prescribing remedies for them, it gave him a credibility that was not entirely deserved. Odum's sleight of hand was surprisingly successful. Donald Davidson, the Vanderbilt Agrarian I mentioned earlier, was one of the few people to catch him at it. In *An American Dilemma,* Gunnar Myrdal did something very similar, as David Southern has shown in a recent study, and Myrdal pretty much got away with it, too. In both cases, I suspect, progressive journalists, clergymen, and academics welcomed "scientific" support for conclusions they were already predisposed to accept—ideas whose time had come—and they were not inclined to look too closely at the value-bridged gap between facts and policy.

Be that as it may, Odum's detailed, exhaustive fact-gathering in *Southern Regions* and elsewhere, supplemented by the similar work of his students, helped to make the South of the 1930s probably the most thoroughly documented society that has ever existed. Historians of the twentieth-century South will always be in the regionalists' debt. Just for example, look at a splendid 1987 book by Jack Temple Kirby, *Rural Worlds Lost,* subtitled *The American South, 1920– 1960*—something of a sequel to Rupert Vance's *Human Geography of the South,* published in 1932.

It is no accident that the golden anniversary of Odum's *Southern Regions,* which passed almost unobserved by the Southern Sociological Society, was marked by a well-attended session at the annual meeting of the Southern Historical Association. By collecting the raw material for Southern historians, Odum and his colleagues became raw material themselves. The reductio ad (almost) absurdum is Wayne Brazil's Harvard dissertation on Odum, which takes nearly seven hundred pages to bring his story up to 1930. But ask yourselves what sociologist of today will be the subject of dissertations in history, much less of prize-winning biographical studies like Daniel Singal's, fifty years from now?

We have this anomaly: regional sociologists are now apparently better known and more respected outside their own discipline than in it. I used the *Social Science Citation Index* and the *Arts & Humanities Citation Index* to look up citations from 1985 and 1986 to the work of five scholars who would make anyone's list of Southern regionalists: Odum himself, Rupert Vance, Guy Johnson, Harriet Herring, and Katherine Jocher. Consider this partial list of journals in which they were cited. (Although such a list is very much in the Odum tradition, do not just sit back and let the poetry of these names wash over you. Notice the diversity of the fields that acknowledge the work of these men and women.)

American Historical Review
Journal of Social History
Journal of Southern History
Journal of Economic History
Journal of Family History
Journal of Library History

American Quarterly
American Speech

Church History
Review of Religious Research

Cornell Law Review
Michigan Law Review
Vanderbilt Law Review
Texas Law Review

Appalachian Journal
Phylon
Journal of Black Studies

Geoform
Geographical Review

Journal of Labor Economics
Explorations in Economic History
Public Administration Review

Urban Affairs Quarterly
Journal of Social, Political and Economic Studies

Journal of Broadcasting and Electronic Media
Critical Studies in Mass Communication

If we ask who appreciates the regionalists these days and why, we discover some pungent ironies. Not least of them is that some of the most discerning recent attention to regionalist thought has come from the Marxist left. (Incidentally, that is true for the proslavery theorists, too.) The most generous assessment of Odum's continuing relevance I have seen lately, for example, is in a 1987 book by a radical economist, Ann Markusen, called *Regions: The Economics and Politics of Territory.*

Left-wing affection for the regionalists may surprise those who know that Odum in particular fell into disfavor with the left in the 1960s and 1970s. He was criticized essentially for being a man of his time and place, and for trying to reform the South from within, rather than seeking root-and-branch transformation. Those of us who found that complaint both anachronistic and utopian are delighted to see these critics outflanked on the left.

To be sure, there is a sense in which Odum's social thought, like that of Henry Hughes and George Fitzhugh, was profoundly conservative. In his own time, however, Odum was continually in hot water for many alleged offenses and some real ones against the South's reigning orthodoxies. From the early 1920s, when the editor of the *Southern Textile Bulletin* accused him of turning the University of North Carolina into "a breeding place for socialism and communism," through the 1940s, when *Southern Regions* was banned in Georgia's public schools, many of Odum's fellow Southerners damned him as a dangerous radical. It is good to see some latter-day radicals appreciating him, even if he was not really one of their own.

Politics aside, though, why should Marxists find regional sociology congenial? I suspect because it dealt with what is a particularly thorny theoretical problem for Marxists, and did so from a perspective basically materialist. As the *Review of Radical Political Economics* put it a while back, "A spectre is haunting socialism—the spectre of regionalism." It is no accident, as Marxists like to say, that the special issue in which those words appeared examined Wales, Galicia, Canada's Maritime Provinces—and the American South. Rupert Vance's circumspect discussion in *Human Geography of the South* of the region's "colonial economy" plainly anticipated what came to be known some decades later as dependency theory.

The regionalists were ahead of their time in some other respects, too. A few years ago I had a letter from a graduate student in American history at Harvard, who was doing her dissertation on the Southern Gulf Coast. She was a fan of Ladurie and Braudel and the other twentieth-century French "scientific historians," and she had just discovered Howard Odum. "Since I'm paying close attention to [Braudel's] writings," she wrote, "I was struck by the similarity in technique between him and Howard Odum. Braudel [also] has a phenomenal mastery of detail over his historical subject, and the same attention to sketching 'portraitures.'"

How about that? If we recognize Odum's interest in what is nowadays called "mentalité" and throw in a reference to Geertzian "thick description," all of a sudden we are looking at an oddly fashionable figure, almost a trendy one. If, as Daniel Singal asserts, Odum was a "modernist [only] by the skin of his teeth," maybe our postmodern age is ready for a reassessment of the man.

There is another irony here, though. Surely, Odum and his colleagues would be gratified to know that Southern historians are still making use of their work decades after it was done. And they would be pleased that their accomplishments are appreciated by many other disciplines; they were *interdisciplinary* before that word became magical. But they would be distressed to see how little they have bequeathed to their own discipline, and in fact Rupert Vance was already distressed in 1960 when he anticipated that outcome, criticizing himself and his colleagues for being better at relating their work to other disciplines than to sociology.

Now, as Vance recognized, this is not sociology's fault. Like any discipline, it has its own criteria of relevance, and, frankly, most of the work identified as "regional sociology" is hardly *sociology* at all, as we understand that word today. But that work can serve to remind us of what we have given up to arrive at that understanding.

Can it be that we have given up too much? Should we think about bringing the regional sociologists' kind of work back into our disciplinary tent? Those questions are beyond my brief for this essay, but to say that this work is not sociology—even to say that it *should* not be—is not to say that it is poor intellectual craftsmanship. The regionalists' work is a gift from Southern sociology to the broader intellectual community, and it seems that other disciplines find it at least as valuable as anything else we have ever given them.

Rupert B. Vance
An Appreciation
with Daniel Joseph Singal

Rupert B. Vance was born in Plummerville, Arkansas, in the closing months of the nineteenth century. He died in Chapel Hill, North Carolina, three-quarters of the way through the twentieth. For him, the South was always home, and in his lifetime he saw the region transformed.

Vance's birthplace was a region still recovering from the Civil War. Its white citizens were suffering the consequences of defeat, occupation, and exploitation, and were engaged in inflicting some of the same experiences on Southern blacks. In 1900, close to 90 percent of Vance's fellow Southerners lived in the countryside, and the region's cities, with a couple of exceptions, did not amount to much. The vast majority of Southerners were farmers and farm workers; nearly all were supported, directly or indirectly, by agriculture. They were supported, as Louis XIV once put it, the way a hanged man is supported by the rope. Southern personal income, per capita, was roughly at the level of Trinidad's today—and was considerably less than half of that in the rest of the United States. Southerners, both black and white, were leaving the region in increasing numbers for employment, or the chance of it, elsewhere. When Vance was born, Southern state legislatures were busy transforming discriminatory custom into the formidable structure of Jim Crow law, designed to fix the Negro "in his place" for eternity. Informal efforts to the same end were commonplace: blacks were being lynched at an average rate of two a week.

When Vance died, his adopted hometown had a black mayor, who was soon to take a cabinet position in the state government of North Carolina. Within a year, the Democratic party would nominate for president a former governor of Georgia, a "born-again" peanut farmer–businessman, backed by Southerners of both races and a good many non-Southerners as well. From the political left came warnings of a sinister entity called the "Sun Belt": this region, which combined the South and Southwest, was alleged to be draining population, wealth, and influence from the old Northeast and achieving a baleful dominance in national affairs from a base of "agribusiness" and extractive industry. Certainly the flow of population had reversed—more blacks and whites were moving to the South than were leaving it—and if per capita income in the South was still lower than that in the rest of the country, the gap had narrowed substantially. In absolute terms the great majority of Southerners led comfortable lives. Like the rest of the United States, the region had become an urban society. By 1975, less than a third of its people were rural, and fewer than one in a dozen actually worked in agriculture. For better or for worse, Atlanta had become the model of the "New South," a hackneyed phrase popularized by an Atlantan over a century before.

Rupert Vance came to Chapel Hill in 1926 to join the Department of Sociology and the Institute for Research in Social Science at the University of North Carolina, both of which had been founded a few years earlier by Howard W. Odum. For the next half century, the South, its problems, and the changes taking place there occupied much of his attention. In a half-dozen books and scores of articles, in his classroom teaching and his work with graduate students, in lectures to varied audiences throughout the South and beyond, Vance applied his intellect and the tools of his discipline to the problems of his native region and, with Odum and his other colleagues, developed the intellectual apparatus of "regional sociology."

Although Vance is probably best known as a student of the South, he easily ranked among the leading sociologists of his generation not only in the South but in the nation and, for that matter, in the world. In 1944, he was elected president of the American Sociological Society (now Association). The depth, quality, and encyclopedic range of his work set a standard for Southern sociologists that has never been equaled.

The breadth of his interests was especially striking. He began by writing the definitive study of the South's cotton tenancy system, moved on to a magisterial portrait of the region from the standpoint of human geography, then to studies of its complex population problems, and finally to examinations of the process that had transformed it from an agricultural to an urban and industrial society. Along the way, he found time to compose remarkably insightful essays on the South's politics, culture, and history, as well as more general contributions to sociological and demographic theory. Unlike the work of many scholars, Vance's has never seemed dated: his masterpiece, *Human Geography of the South,* can be read with almost as much profit today as when it first appeared in 1932. His accomplishments also included over forty years of teaching and directing graduate studies at the University of North Carolina in Chapel Hill, where he was made Kenan Professor of Sociology in 1946, and service as a consultant to innumerable government commissions and agencies and to the United Nations (on international migration).

Vance's achievement is all the more noteworthy because he worked throughout his career with a severe physical handicap. Born in 1899 in a small central Arkansas town, he contracted polio at the age of three and soon lost the use of both legs. Unable to obtain treatment or even proper diagnosis in his hometown—"It was hell to live in the backwoods then," he would later recall—he and his mother spent two years at the McLean Orthopedic Hospital in St. Louis, where he learned to walk with the aid of crutches. Although the affliction kept him from entering school until age ten, he was able to enter in the fourth grade and promptly rose to the top of the class; thereafter, his paralysis had no significant effects on either his education or his career. Colleagues would later marvel at how Vance kept up a full round of professional activities, including a busy schedule of travel to meetings and conferences. Nor did his handicap exclude him from the normal boyhood pastimes: a 1950 profile in the *Raleigh News and Observer* reported that he often served as umpire for youngsters' baseball games. "He stood on crutches behind the pitcher," it noted, "and he never reversed a decision."

Like his mentor Odum, Vance grew up in a rural community typical of the South in that day. His grandfather was a Confederate veteran; his father a New South–style cotton planter, who managed his work force of sharecroppers from behind the counter of his general store. Several times, the elder Vance tried to escape the narrow confines of the cotton system by raising peaches, cantaloupes, or livestock, but each time the vicissitudes of the national market brought financial disaster. His efforts to prosper growing cotton also met repeated failure owing to the sharp fluctuations in the price of that staple. During the agricultural depression of the early 1920s, he finally went bankrupt and lost all his land. To his son this spectacle of hard work and initiative culminating in failure came to epitomize the overall plight of the South. Why, he asked himself, were capable Southerners like his father forever frustrated in their desire to improve themselves? Was something grievously wrong with the South's culture, or economy, or social system, or perhaps with the genetic makeup of its people?

His education had given him a broad background to draw upon in his search for an answer. Taught to read at age four by his mother, he soon developed an appetite for books that his family found hard to satisfy, even though they purchased Dickens, Irving, and Scott by the set. The results of this early exposure were later reflected in his own writing, which was always clear (and not just "for a sociologist") and often elegant. He attended college at Henderson Brown, a small Methodist school in Arkadelphia, where he edited the college paper and yearbook, was president of the Young Men's Christian Association, and served as class valedictorian. Although he majored in English, his first love, he also encountered a gifted teacher named B. S. Foster who introduced him to social science. Intrigued by the new field, he accepted a scholarship to Vanderbilt to study for a master's degree in economics. His studies there with Augustus Dyer, a stodgy and resolute exponent of classical laissez-faire, left him with little taste for economics unleavened by sociological analysis. He found the double-distilled Southern progressivism of Edward Mims (later to write *The Advancing South*) more attractive, though, and he was exposed to such fellow students as Ralph McGill (about whom he was later to tell some hilarious stories) and some young literati who were later to number among the Vanderbilt Agrarians.

After Vanderbilt, still unsure of his choice of profession and unwilling to enter law school (as his father advised), Vance entered a period of apparent drift, but one in which his social views were in actuality maturing rapidly. He took a job for two years as principal of a small Oklahoma high school and then taught English for three years at South Georgia College in McRae.

Vance later attributed much importance to his time in McRae. His social views were developing, he recognized, in a liberal direction, and while they had been fairly unremarkable in the Southwest and at Vanderbilt, they were enough out of place in south Georgia that his colleagues sometimes accused him of being a disguised Yankee. (This experience almost certainly had something to do with his lifelong interest in subregional differences, an interest he turned to good account in his *Human Geography of the South.*)

All the while, he was avidly reading many books and periodicals, especially H. L. Mencken's iconoclastic *American Mercury.* (Until he met Mencken, Vance said, he had always assumed that the man ate little children for breakfast.) It was during this period that he also discovered Howard Odum's *Journal of Social Forces,* with its hard-hitting editorials cataloging the South's ills and proposing programs of action to address them. This kind of engagé academic sociology appealed to Vance because it provided a way both to implement his commitment to reform and to satisfy his intellectual curiosity. After considering Columbia University and Chicago, he chose Chapel Hill as the place to do his graduate work, primarily because of the chance to work with Odum.

A young and energetic Southern-born sociologist, Odum had come to Chapel Hill in 1920 to found an academic empire. He came as first director of the university's School of Public Welfare and as chairman of its new sociology department (the only one in the South). Two years later he began the *Journal of Social Forces,* with himself as editor, and in 1924, with support from the Laura Spelman Rockefeller Memorial, launched the Institute for Research in Social Science. His two basic goals were closely related: he wished to promote the scientific study of Southern society so that people in the region could begin tackling their immense problems in constructive ways, and he hoped to provide an opportunity for talented Southerners to train in the new social science disciplines unhampered by financial cares or constraints on their freedom of inquiry. To those ends, the institute offered fellowships to promising graduate students willing to investigate aspects of Southern life. The stipends were high, the length of tenure was open, and there was no obligation to teach. Vance was one of the first to take advantage of these attractive terms, and so began an extraordinary association that was to last until Odum's death nearly thirty years later.

Odum was in his early forties when Vance came to Chapel Hill at age twenty-seven, and from the start relations between the two men were warm and mutually admiring. Keenly aware of Odum's sensitivities, Vance always maintained the humble role of student, of the loyal disciple both grateful to and slightly in awe of his master. And there was much to be grateful for. Odum provided Vance not only with institutional support and personal encouragement but, just as importantly, with the drive to theorize and to generalize that would ultimately raise Vance's work well above simple description. In addition, Odum reinforced Vance's sense of mission about the South, an unapologetic assumption that something *must be done* about the problems they were studying. Vance always acknowledged his intellectual debt to Odum: one of his last published articles was, in effect, an act of homage to his mentor, an attempt to restore one of Odum's neglected concepts to use. For his part, Vance contributed as much as anyone to realizing Odum's vision of Chapel Hill as a center of regional scholarship and what is now called "policy research." In both volume and quality, his publications helped put North Carolina on the national academic map.

Yet Vance proved to be different in many ways, both temperamentally and intellectually, from his master. Odum's training had been in the organicist brand of sociology that was dominant before World War I. As a result, he tended to view the ideal society as a seamless web in which all groups and social institutions functioned harmoniously with one another. Odum regarded any sign of conflict as aberrational and potentially dangerous—political conflict as the worst. Thus, his ideology of "regionalism" included a blueprint for Southern society in which consensus was so strong that the projects of academic social planners and the desires of the common folk would be instantly and automatically reconciled.

More solidly grounded in the newer developments in social science, Vance had no such illusions. For him, conflict was at least a given, if not a positive good, as evidenced by a memorandum he wrote to Odum after reading the manuscript of Odum's *American Regionalism:*

> I believe I must be wanting a more hard-boiled view of social conflict. Conflict we will always have with us. How does Regionalism take [sectional conflict] out of the realm of hard knocks and place it in the realm of discussion and reasonable "due process" of policy-making? And what about class conflict? . . . Maybe it comes down to this, that we can't take a point of view without taking sides. Still, I have the feeling that we need to be sure of the alternatives, if necessary to argue one side and then the other, show the interest involved.

Vance's graduate school paper on "Stuart-Harmon" (a thinly disguised picture of McRae, Georgia) contains a forthright treatment of class, racial, and generational conflict, and his dissertation, while it makes a scapegoat of no one, nevertheless recognizes that tenant and landlord necessarily have some divergent interests.[1]

Vance's fascination with Southern politics, a subject not for those squeamish about conflict and one that Odum largely ignored in his own work, led him to undertake a series of articles on populist-style Southern politicians, beginning with a sketch of Jeff Davis of Arkansas entitled "A Karl Marx for Hill Billies," published in *Social Forces* in 1930. This article, perhaps more than any other, shows Mencken's influence. Vance was not the only reform-minded young Southerner to read the *American Mercury;* as Fred C. Hobson, Jr., has pointed out, Mencken was something of a hero to many. Having

---

1. Vance's major papers and articles on the South have been collected in Reed and Singal, eds., *Regionalism and the South.*

flayed the South in his famous essay "Sahara of the Bozart," Mencken was encouraging those Southerners who were trying to remedy the situation that he had (exaggeratedly) diagnosed, and he published works by many of them in his magazine. His relations with Odum and his students were warm and supportive, and Vance admitted in later years that his piece on Jeff Davis was written with the *American Mercury* in mind. Still, it appeared in Odum's journal, not Mencken's.

Vance also differed from Odum in the style and approach of his writings. What someone once said of Kant could be said as well of Odum: he was both like and unlike Jehovah—he spoke through a cloud, but without the illumination of the thunderbolt. Vance's work, on the other hand, was always lucid and well organized, proceeding through clear-cut logical analysis to an identifiable conclusion. In some ways, Vance served as an interpreter for Odum, by clarifying and substantiating the latter's ideas on regionalism, making them comprehensible to readers who could not pin Odum down in person for an explanation. On at least one occasion, Vance even tried valiantly to repair Odum's prose, after plowing through the draft of a 1938 book:

> My first impression [wrote the former English teacher] was that the materials were undigested and the manuscript was rather hastily done. [For example,] I look for a resolution, a point of view or a summary at the end of many chapters, and I find sometimes an abrupt conclusion and sometimes a quotation. . . . I would like to see [in] the manuscript the emergence of what might be called a point of view. Some of the most original and challenging of your ideas are stated as assumptions rather than emerging from the discussions as conclusions. Again, I see certain slants that are taken without being explicitly defined or argued.

This memorandum (which goes on) tells us something of the nature of the relationship between the two men. So may the fact that Odum apparently left the manuscript unrevised.

These contrasts between the two were apparent in Vance's *Human Factors in Cotton Culture,* a revised version of his doctoral dissertation published in 1929. Whereas Odum's writing on the South tended to be upbeat and optimistic, Vance's portrait of how Southerners were trapped by what he called "the cotton culture complex" was strongly pessimistic. Ever mindful of his father's experience, he stressed the ruinous unpredictability of the system by emphasizing how the cycles of the cotton market or the vagaries of the weather could destroy men's livelihoods virtually overnight and lead them to irrational behavior. He employed statistics and graphic literary detail to depict the lives of ordinary tenant farmers, again drawing on his personal recollections, and presented anything but a pretty picture. The resulting book was, as one reviewer aptly put it, "a rare combination of sound economics and human interest."

The book eschewed easy solutions. Far from holding out hope for reform, Vance concluded that the dependence on King Cotton led to a "vicious circle" almost impossible to break, a system whose participants "form an economic harmony that often benefits all except the producer, a complex whole that is so closely interconnected that no one can suggest any place at which it may be attacked except the grower; and the grower is to change the system himself, cold comfort for advice." The book introduced a needed note of sober realism to subsequent discussions of the South's problems in the 1930s.

Still, in *Human Factors,* Vance did not really answer his basic causal question of what had gone wrong in the South; that answer came in his *Human Geography of the South,* which appeared in 1932. This massive work, with a bibliography long enough to impress even the most compulsive scholar, surely belongs among the classics of American social science. Borrowing techniques from the French school of human geographers and from the new science of ecology, Vance tried to see if some natural factor—some inescapable attribute of the physical environment—could account for the ills of Southern life. Methodically, he reviewed the region's physical features as they had interacted with its social development, only to conclude that all, from topography and soil content to water supplies, had been sufficient for prosperity. An especially provocative chapter on the Southern climate showed that, if anything, the region's weather should have given it a clear advantage over the North in industrial production. Chapters on the supposed biological inferiority of the Southern people demonstrated that what many observers had described as "laziness" could more accurately be attributed to inadequate diets and endemic diseases like hookworm and malaria. The South's plight was not the fault of nature, then, but was in fact man-made. Natural forces may have played a role, but in the end, Vance insisted, "history, not geography, made the solid South."

More precisely, according to Vance, history had left Southern society arrested in the frontier stage. Adapting his thesis from the work of the historian Ulrich B. Phillips—whose influence on Vance was second only to that of Odum—he maintained that the social and economic patterns of the South had been shaped essentially by the plantation, a frontier institution that produced cotton by almost literally mining the soil. During the nineteenth century, the rest of the country shed its colonial status as an exporter of raw materials to become an industrial society. Because of its dependence on the plantation system and, later, the devastation of the Civil War, the South failed to keep pace. The region never built up a capital supply of its own and remained backward in technology and industrial skills. The result, Vance argued, was a "colonial economy" frantically exploiting its natural resources to pay for manufactured goods produced elsewhere. The North (he quickly added) was not to blame; rather, the tragic course of Southern history had condemned the region to its poverty and dependence. To escape this fate, Vance believed, Southerners would have to strive consciously for urbanization and industrialization and for a more diversified agricultural system that was less dependent on staple crops. More cautiously than Odum, he endorsed regional planning as the quickest and most efficient route to a mature economy, but he characteristically pointed out that any such program would have to take into account the entrenched folkways of a people still under the sway of the plantation mentality.

The publication of *Human Geography of the South* cemented Vance's reputation as a leading figure in sociology. Invitations began pouring in for him to serve as consultant on various projects, both scholarly and governmental, and Vance was usually quick to take them up. He actively lobbied for passage of the Bankhead-Jones Farm Tenant Bill and, after its enactment in 1938, frequently acted as advisor to the Farm Security Administration, which was created by the new law. In addition, he was among the founders of the Southern Sociological Society in 1935 and became its third president in 1938. His most important contribution to the organization, he liked to recall afterward, was seeing to it that the society met from the start only in hotels where its black members could attend all functions, including formal dinners. Finding such facilities in the South of the 1930s was not always easy, but Vance and others persisted in this policy, with the result that some other professional associations then getting under way in the region followed suit.

At the same time, Vance was becoming increasingly interested in the fledgling field of social demography. In 1938 he published a *Research Memorandum on Population Redistribution within the United States,* for the Social Science Research Council, attempting to set forth an agenda for research in an area whose importance was just beginning to be recognized by sociologists generally.

In fact, by the mid-1930s Vance had begun to view population as an alternative explanation of the South's dilemma. The solid, scientific feel of demographic theory strongly appealed to him; it was hard to argue against numbers. More important, as Vance was to demonstrate in *All these People: The Nation's Human Resources in the South* (his next major study, published in 1945), there could be no question that the South since the Civil War had been dramatically overproducing people. Again the fault seemed to lie with the system of staple crop agriculture, which encouraged families to have as many children as possible in order to have hands available for field labor. But, as Vance showed, whatever the short-run advantages for individual families, this system led to long-run disadvantages for the region and nation, since the huge reservoir of underemployed workers that resulted kept wages in the South at a bare subsistence level. Here, Vance thought, was the root cause of Southern poverty. His solution once more was an industrialized and urbanized society, arrived at through planning, precisely because urban life and higher living standards would of themselves help to lower the birthrate and thus to solve the South's population problem. He had only limited faith, however, that such planning would actually come about. More realistically, as early as his 1936 article "The Old Cotton Belt," Vance foresaw the process in which the South would export its surplus population to the urban slums of the North, with tragic consequences for the country as a whole.

Vance continued his interest in demography, becoming president of the Population Association of America in 1952, but in the latter part of his career he focused his attention primarily on the subject of urbanization itself. In a 1955 article he claimed, accurately as it turned out, that a major "breakthrough" had taken place in the South around the middle of the preceding decade: the cities rather than the country-side had finally come to dominate the society. For Vance, the main significance of this development was its meaning for the South's relationship to the rest of the nation. As he observed in *The Urban South,* a symposium he edited at this time with a Chapel Hill colleague, Nicholas Demerath, the South in one critical area after another was finally catching up with the other regions. The indices of Southern deficiency that he and Odum had charted for years were at last disappearing. Put another way, the circumstances that had prevented members of his father's generation from succeeding, despite their best efforts, appeared to be past.

Although this view was correct as far as it went, it clearly failed to take into account the other major change that was occurring in South-ern life during these years, namely, the civil rights movement, which in 1954 and 1955 saw both the Supreme Court decision in *Brown v. Board of Education* and the Montgomery bus boycott. Vance may well have hesitated to trespass in an area he regarded as the domain of his friend and colleague Guy Johnson, but in any case, despite his own liberal racial views, the changing structure of Southern race relations simply did not receive the attention in his published work that, in retrospect, it clearly deserves in any account of the South's modernization.

Another difficulty the contemporary reader may find in Vance's work is the concept of regionalism itself. To a greater extent than is usually recognized, Vance was as much the father of regional soci-ology as was Odum. Indeed, Vance's explorations in human geogra-phy, his charting of subregions and resources, led directly to Odum's pointillist portrait of the South in *Southern Regions,* an imposing study published in 1936. Vance was always far more conversant with modern social theory than was his mentor, and the gap between that theory and regionalism troubled him. To the charge that regionalists were engaged in "mere description" of particular locales rather than in the attempt to build a general science of society, Vance replied that description was a necessary preliminary operation: "The truth in the statement I do not find too disturbing provided one can go from description to generalization by good empirical methods. There are certainly sufficient regions and sufficient societies to offer basis for valid generalization." To the accusation that regionalists in attempting to understand a region by dabbling in history, geography, and economics were doing everything *but* sociology, Vance replied ruefully: "I have sometimes said that it must be fun to be a dilettante, but dilettantes are not supposed to work very hard." He added: "Regionalism focuses many disciplines on the one area under study, and anyone who follows this line takes a calculated risk that leads to trespassing on other people's preserves."

Nevertheless, he acknowledged (in a 1948 letter) that "all of these things [his extrasociological interests] have enabled me to examine one region from different facets, but they have not brought me much closer to the core and essence of sociology." This lack of connection still troubled him over a decade later. In 1960, he was writing that "regional sociology has been much better at taking in other people's washing, relating its contributions to those of geography, economics, political science, and so forth than it has been in relating regionalism to its own domain, that of general sociology."

This uneasiness may have been aggravated by the postwar development of the South. Since its origins lay in a concern with the economic and social problems of the region, regionalism faced a dilemma when those problems appeared to be on the way to solution. Vance was delighted with the South's modernization but realized its consequences for his own style of research. As he put it in 1960: "The New Deal has been dealt. . . . As the affluent society crosses the Mason-Dixon line, the regionalist of the 1930s turns up as just another 'liberal without a cause.'" Whatever the reason, it is ironic that by the early 1950s, when Vance produced for a symposium on regionalism what is probably the clearest statement available of what the

regional sociologists were up to, his own work had largely left regionalism behind. As something of a valedictory gesture, although it may
not have been intended as such, he and Charles Grigg presented a
paper to the American Sociological Association in 1956 that proposed a synthesis of the declining subdiscipline of regional sociology
(purged of its particularistic emphasis on the South) and the ascen-
dant one of human ecology. Unlike corporate mergers, intellectual
ones are not a matter of public record, but if this one took place, it
resembled many corporate mergers in that the smaller party effectively vanished. Still, the student of intellectual life who is looking for
regionalism's impact on its parent discipline of sociology must seek it
in the work of present-day human ecologists. If regionalism produced a third generation, it is effectively disguised.

In the years after 1960, however, Vance's attention did return occasionally to the South in papers dealing with aspects of the region's
social structure and "quality of life" more subtle than those linked
directly to per capita income: education, family life, high culture. In
addition, Vance became concerned with Appalachia, largely bypassed
by the urbanization and industrialization that transformed the rest of
the South. Appalachia's problems were much like those of the South
as a whole thirty years earlier and seemed susceptible to study and
treatment in the old regionalist framework.

But if the relation of Vance's interests to one another and to those of
his discipline of sociology occasionally troubled him, it need not
concern his readers. When he "trespassed" on other disciplines, he
did it well, and the natives recognized that. Although he never studied
human geography, population, human ecology, and social structure
in the classroom, his authority in these areas was recognized. Although affiliated with a sociology department, he was always being
mistaken—flatteringly, he said—for something else: "O. E. Baker nomi-
nated me to the Association of American Geographers. . . . Carter
Goodrich thought I was an economist when he asked me to work
with the Study of Population Redistribution. There was a time when
work in tenancy led some to classify me with the rural sociologists.
The editors of the *History of the South* persuaded me to attempt the
last volume for their series [an attempt later abandoned]."

These confusions and problems of classification are testimony to the range of Vance's interests and the caliber of his mind. In his works on the South, we see a vigorous and well-informed intellect addressing some of the most pressing problems of his day. In the works on regionalism, Vance pondered the questions of how to bring together many disciplines without becoming undisciplined altogether, of how to study a region "as a whole" without simply studying *everything*—questions still vital to all interdisciplinary enterprises.

Vance was very much a man of his time. As the citation accompanying his honorary degree from the University of North Carolina accurately observed, he "contributed not only to the understanding of the human problems of this century, particularly those of his native South, but to the solution of many of them." In doing so, however, he also exemplified some virtues of an earlier time. Like others of his colleagues at Chapel Hill, Robert Coles has observed, the "narrative power" of Vance's work carried on "an older tradition of social science, and a Southern one." When Gunnar Myrdal made a related point, in *An American Dilemma,* he undoubtedly had Vance and his colleagues in mind: "Social science in the South has never, as in the North, lost the tradition of reasoning in terms of means and ends. . . . The significance for human happiness of the problems under study is always a present thought in the South."

But if Vance addressed the problems of his day in a style recognized even then as an "older" one, he was also, in an important sense, ahead of his time. Whatever the final verdict on regionalism, Vance's excursions into geography, history, economics, and political science evidence his vision of a unified social science, his conviction that a complicated modern society like the American South cannot rightfully be vivisected for the convenience of academic departments. It is a measure of his foresight that this fact is only now becoming obvious to the rest of us.

For Dixieland
The Sectionalism of *I'll Take My Stand*

A sociologist—particularly a *Chapel Hill* sociologist—must feel some diffidence when discussing the Vanderbilt Agrarians, the Twelve Southerners who wrote *I'll Take My Stand.* As the historian I. A. Newby has written, "Next to Communists and industrialists, the Agrarians considered their chief antagonists to be [the] group of sociologists and regional planners at the University of North Carolina." There is no profit in raking up that old controversy: the Carolinians' prescriptions seem to have carried the day, but it is *I'll Take My Stand,* not Howard Odum's *Southern Regions,* that is still being read after fifty years. You have conquered, O Tennesseans.

Yet such competence as I have is as a sociologist, and I really have nothing to add to what has been said about the Agrarians as literary men. What I propose is to examine them sociologically, as a social movement of a particular sort: not in order to pigeonhole them, not to "explain" and thereby to diminish their achievement, but rather to draw attention to those things that they shared with other, similar movements. Since sociology has its limitations, as Donald Davidson was fond of pointing out, this approach can only make, at best, a limited contribution to understanding a complex movement, comprising a dozen exceedingly complex men.[1] But what a sociologist

1. I recognize the difficulty of generalizing about this group of twelve individualists, and what I have to say will undoubtedly be more true of some than of

28

can do is to observe that, increasingly for the past 200 years and now almost universally, circumstances like those the Twelve Southerners faced have led some people like them to say things like what they said. If the Nashville group said these things better, or said something else besides, a glance at these other similar movements may help us identify what was, in fact, unique about their statement.

One way to look at the Agrarians, and certainly a useful way, places them in a tradition of anti-industrial thought that goes back at least to John Ruskin and Thomas Carlyle and the Maypole-on-the-village-green socialism of William Morris, extends through T. S. Eliot and the English Distributists, and can be found today in the work of such strange bedfellows as Paul Goodman, Ivan Illich, and E. F. Schumacher, with echoes from the former governor of California and the *Mother Earth News.* Among the Agrarians' contemporaries, we can hear similar themes from even such dyed-in-the-wool Yankees as Albert Jay Nock, whose sketch of the imaginary country of "Amenia" resembles the Agrarians' ideal more than incidentally, and Ralph Adams Cram, who had more success reviving Gothic architecture than Gothic thought, but very much admired the neofeudalism of Franklin D. Roosevelt and Benito Mussolini. (Cram's grandfather, to judge from his grandson's portrait, would have hit it off famously with John Donald Wade's Cousin Lucius, for all that the old man was a New Englander.)

But as a specimen of this Anglo-American tradition, the Agrarians' writings were unusual in one very important respect: they did not look back to the Middle Ages or ahead to some envisioned sometime to see the realization of their ideal. No, they claimed that ideal was realized, or had been realized until recently, or perhaps was almost realized—anyway, that it was somehow incarnate right where they took their stand, in the American South. Their manifesto defended a

---

others. The themes I will emphasize can be found in many of the essays in *I'll Take My Stand* and in its introductory statement, but they were developed more fully in the later writings of some of the contributors, notably Donald Davidson and Frank Owsley. Both implied at times that they were speaking for the group, and I shall take them at their word, since only H. C. Nixon saw fit to dissociate himself publicly from what they were saying during the 1930s.

way of life, an economic system they thought was necessary for it, and a particular region they believed embodied it. The South and agriculture seemed at the time to be joined intimately, if not inextricably, and there is no need to say which of the twelve loved the South because it was agrarian and which valued agrarianism because it was the South's way. I doubt that most could have said themselves in 1930, and in any case no one had to say until much later.

But to emphasize an obvious fact that we should not overlook, whatever else *I'll Take My Stand* may be, it is a very *Southern* book. Despite some well-known objections, it was not called *Tracts against Communism* but took its title from the Confederate anthem. The authors were "Twelve Southerners," not Twelve Agrarians, Twelve Anti-Communists, or Twelve Poets. The book begins with the words: "The authors contributing to this book are Southerners." If we can believe some of the contributors, even its intended audience was exclusively Southern.

It is easy to overemphasize this aspect of the manifesto, as did the critic who concluded that the Agrarians' economic ideas were "just a literary device, a periphrastic manner of expressing an emotion," and that, really, agrarianism was "simply the name for a discontent with the contemporary situation in the South." But it is equally wrong-headed to ignore the fact that most of the twelve *were* discontented with that situation, and did mean to grind some axes and air some grievances.

Among us Chapel Hill sociologists, that attitude is known as *sectionalism,* and it made my predecessors, the Agrarians' adversaries, very uncomfortable. But a sociological analysis of *I'll Take My Stand* requires that we look at this aspect of it, and not just with alarm. A theory of sectionalism would help, but there is no such creature. There is another word, though, and a body of theory to go with it, for movements that seek to attain and to defend the integrity and the interests of ethnic or regional groups. Elsewhere in the world, we call that *nationalism.*[2]

2. Nationalism is often understood to imply a program of political independence for the alleged nation, but that is not a necessary or defining characteris-

That is the off-the-rack sociological category I want to measure the Agrarians for in this essay. Twenty years after *I'll Take My Stand,* Frank Owsley made my point better than I possibly could. "There is no question," he said, "that much of the bitter resentment of backward peoples in the Orient against, what they term . . . 'Yankee imperialism' is similar to that felt by the contributors to *I'll Take My Stand* in 1930." To understand the book, he insisted, it is necessary to recognize that it was not just a protest against industrialism, but equally a protest against the North's "brazen and contemptuous treatment" of the South "as a colony and as a conquered province."

If we ask what else the Agrarians had in common with those backward anticolonialists in the Orient, and with other nationalists from Quebec to Kurdistan, if we examine *I'll Take My Stand* in the light of nationalist manifestoes from around the world, the similarities are obvious. Consider first this business of grievances. Sheldon Hackney has written that there is a sense of grievance at the heart of Southern identity, and if he is right, there is no question that *I'll Take My Stand* is a very Southern book in this respect as well.

The most obvious grievance was a cultural one. The Agrarians were not altogether persuasive, clear, or even agreed about what the South's culture was (who ever has been, for that matter?), but they did believe it was both threatened and looked down on by the rest of the United States, and by the industrial Northeast in particular. Whether or not the genesis of the movement is actually to be found in the Dayton "Monkey Trial," as some of the contributors said, certainly the South had a bad press throughout the 1920s, and these men were well aware of it. In a later essay, for example, Donald Davidson sketched what he took to be the characteristic view of the South from New York: "a region full of little else but lynchings, shootings, chain gangs, poor whites, Ku Kluxers, hookworm, pellagra, and a few decayed patri-

---

tic. Consider, for example, Flemish nationalism, which seeks protection and autonomy within Belgium, not independence from it. Cultural nationalism may develop into a movement for political independence, but even if that is the usual process, it is not an inevitable one. In any case, as I shall show, the "sectionalism" of the Agrarians did not rule out the demand for some indeterminate measure of political autonomy for the South.

cians whose chief intent is to deprive the uncontaminated, spiritual-singing Negro of his life and liberty." In *I'll Take My Stand* itself, Frank Owsley protested the smug prejudice of the North, which "still sits in Pharisaical judgment upon the South, beating its chest and thanking-Thee-O-Lord-that-I-am-not-as-other-men." John Crowe Ransom, for his part, lamented that the unreconstructed Southerner was regarded as "quaint" and "eccentric"—"a rare exhibit in the antique kind [whose] position is secure from the interference of the police . . . but is of a rather ambiguous dignity."

The Agrarians were especially alarmed that Southerners were in danger of absorbing Northern views of their own history and culture. Allen Tate complained that things had reached the point where "Southern school children sing 'Land of the Pilgrims' Pride.'" Davidson criticized Northern textbooks and models for "uprooting" Southern students, and Owsley's description of the "war of intellectual and spiritual conquest" against the South deserves to be quoted at length:

> The rising generations read Northern literature, shot through with the New England tradition. Northern textbooks were used in Southern schools . . . —books that were built around the Northern legend and either completely ignored the South or insisted upon the unrighteousness of most of its history and its philosophy of life. One would judge . . . that the Puritans and Pilgrim fathers were the ancestors of every self-respecting American. Southern children spoke of "our Puritan fathers." . . . As time rolled on, the chorus of "John Brown's Body" swelled ever louder and louder until the lusty voices of grandchildren and great-grandchildren of rebels joined in the singing.

I'll Take My Stand was clearly meant to be the opening salvo of a counterattack in this spiritual and intellectual war. For Owsley, the professional historian, the task seemed straightforward, if not easy. The "crusade being levelled against the South," he said later, was "based on poor information, or bad reporting"; so "to aid the South in its reorientation and in a return to its true philosophy"—the purpose, he said, of *I'll Take My Stand*—it was simply a matter of setting the record straight.

For some of the other contributors, the relation of the countermyth they were constructing to the South's actual history was a bit more . . . subtle. Ransom's thoughts on the utility of myth had been a matter of record since his unorthodox defense of fundamentalist religion in *God without Thunder,* and in *I'll Take My Stand* he not only acknowledged that "there are a good many faults to be found with the old South" but allowed that "it does not greatly matter to what extent the identical features of the old Southern establishment are restored," so long as there was an "establishment" of *some* sort, "for the sake of stability." Stark Young went even further: "Dead days are gone," he wrote, "and if by some chance they should return, we should find them intolerable." The task, in his view, was to develop "some conception of the end of living, the civilization, that will belong to the South." As for academic history—well, Young felt there was something to be said for believing even "lies" if their effect on conduct was uplifting.

All in all, for men widely believed to be defending the Southern tradition, some of the twelve took a curiously insouciant attitude toward what it might actually be. Some of the others explicitly regretted parts of it: Tate, for instance, was clearly distressed that the South's religious tradition is what it is (hardly a traditionalist view in the ordinary sense of that word), while Henry Blue Kline apparently rejected even the *agrarian* component of the Southern tradition, saying that he would "resist any tendency to go too far back to the soil."

But whatever the content of the countermyth was to be, whatever its relation to the actual facts of Southern history and culture, the essayists of *I'll Take My Stand* wanted to forge a view of the South's past and its future that Southerners did not have to be ashamed of, one that might even win some respect outside the region. Most were trying to be faithful to the facts, and the facts were that the great *differentiae* of the South were three—three Rs, as it happens: race, religion, and rural life. On all three scores, the Agrarians recognized that the South was seen as backward and "un-American."

Oddly, perhaps, given the time and place, they largely ignored race. When it was mentioned, it was often (as in Robert Penn Warren's essay) in rather untraditional terms. I suppose that all of them were at the time segregationists, but that is beside the point. They did not base their defense of the South on its undeniable standing as the last great Western Hemisphere redoubt of white supremacy. (Other spokesmen for the South have not shared their scruples, or their tact.) Their defense of the South emphasized the last two of those three Rs—religion and, especially, rural life. They effected a sort of rhetorical alchemy, transmuting vice into virtue, proclaiming that backward is beautiful. And some of us think they did it very persuasively.

I do not suggest that this choice of a myth—this choice, in a way, of a tradition—was merely rhetorical, still less that it was arbitrary or cynical. For most of the twelve, I am sure, the revulsion at industrialism and secularism and all of the related "isms" was genuine and visceral. But this defense of a way of life for which they adopted the shorthand label *agrarian* did have rhetorically useful consequences. In particular, it supplied a solution to the problem of dignity with which the Agrarians, as Southerners, were concerned. It even suggested that the South might be a beacon, an example for the rest of the world to emulate.

But the Agrarians not only wanted to identify and to refurbish the Southern tradition, or anyway *a* Southern tradition, they also meant to defend it—and if it was indeed linked to agriculture and rural life, it greatly needed defense. The spread of industrialism menaced those aspects of Southern life, and, some of the twelve came to believe, its dominance debased them. So here was an economic grievance to add to the cultural one. The Agrarians argued only that farming *could* be an ennobling way of life. They were not naive or stupid, and they recognized that it takes a great deal to ennoble someone who is underfed and shackled with debt. As Ransom put it: "Unregenerate Southerners were trying to live the good life on a shabby equipment, and they were grotesque in their effort to make an art out of living when they were not decently making the living."

In *I'll Take My Stand,* most were unclear about why this situation existed, although they seemed to agree that Appomattox had something to do with it. (Ransom came perilously close to attributing it to defect of character.) After the book appeared, perhaps in response to those who sneered at their ignorance of economics, several of the twelve undertook to learn something of the subject, and their diagnosis later became much more sophisticated: they began to write knowledgeably about tariffs, about patterns of ownership and tenure, about property taxes, freight rate differentials, and international markets. Their generalized suspicion that somehow the North was to blame for the South's problems was elaborated into a full-fledged analysis of the South's "colonial economy."[3]

They began also to suggest programs. Lyle Lanier proposed to nationalize large, multiregional industries; Tate suggested worker control on what would later be called the "Yugoslavian" model; Davidson discussed what could be done with reform of corporate profits taxes; and Owsley, in an essay he said had been approved by "quite a number" of the twelve, outlined a plan of agrarian reform and redistribution that earned from one critic the label *kremlinesque* (although Owsley didn't go as far as W. T. Couch of Chapel Hill, who thought collective farms might be a good idea for the South).

But, as some realized from the start, to implement these or any other reforms required power, a degree of self-determination the South had not had since 1865. As the Agrarians saw it, the South existed within a federal system dominated by the industrial interests of the Northeast. Why should those interests voluntarily acquiesce in attempts to limit their power? In the "colonial economy" view of things, why should they do anything for the South? They had an interest in keeping it a hinterland too poor to industrialize on its own, a supplier of raw materials, a good place to put branch factories that needed only unskilled labor, and (behind tariff walls) a captive market. So add to the economic and cultural grievances a political one.

It was all very well for the introductory statement in *I'll Take My Stand* to say that "the South [proposes] to determine itself" in order to protect its "minority right to live its own kind of life." But the mani-

---

3. I am almost certain that this analysis was taken over intact from a book published shortly after *I'll Take My Stand* by Rupert Vance, one of those Chapel Hill sociologists. Vance seldom used the phrase *colonial economy* again and largely avoided the subject altogether. When I asked him why, he told me that his analysis gave aid and comfort to "sectionalists." But he never said his analysis was *wrong*.

festo said almost nothing about the form that self-determination was to take or how it was to be achieved. Kline suggested economic boycotts and some sort of unspecified "civic and political activity" to discourage "promoters and exploiters"; Tate unhappily allowed that the only solution was "political, active, and, in the nature of the case, violent and revolutionary"; and Ransom suggested that if the South and its allies could not achieve a position of dominance within the Union, then a "nasty" agitprop campaign, portraying industrialism as "a foreign invasion of Southern soil," might secure for the South "a position in the Union analogous more or less to the position of Scotland under the British crown—a section with a very local and peculiar culture that would, nevertheless, be secure and respected."

But like the Scottish nationalists, some of the Agrarians came to believe that toleration was not sufficient. Both Davidson (in *Who Owns America?*) and Owsley (in that essay approved by "quite a number" of the others) proposed what the British now call "devolution"—"a new constitutional deal," in Owsley's words, that would put most of the domestic functions of government in the hands of the regions.

From time to time, spokesmen for the Agrarians denied that they were rethinking secession, but some denied it rather unconvincingly. Both Owsley and Davidson, for instance, warned that something like their plan for regional autonomy was required if the United States was to endure. Davidson imagined some future historian lecturing on the 1930s, pausing to say "with emphasis" (and Davidson put these lines in italics): *"At this point regional differences passed beyond the possibility of adjustment under the Federal system, and here, therefore, began the dismemberment of the United States, long since foreshadowed in the struggles of the eighteen-sixties."* I cannot say how genuine was his distress at that prospect.[4]

4. In much of this, there was an element of posturing, even of playfulness, that makes it difficult to say how serious the Agrarians were, but some were obviously more serious than others. (Ransom wrote to Tate in 1932, "You know, our rebel doctrines are good for all of us but Don, and very doubtful there, because they are flames to his tinder.") The same spirit can be observed, and the same difficulty arises, in the early stages of similar movements—Scottish, Quebecois, or Occitanian nationalism, for instance.

In any case, we find in *I'll Take My Stand* all of the characteristic grievances—cultural, economic, and political—of a typical national-ist movement. And, especially if we follow the Agrarians past *I'll Take My Stand,* we find more than glimmerings of the typical nationalist responses: cultural defense, economic autarky, even political self-determination.

So what? What profit is there in putting Ransom, Davidson, and the others in a category that includes Herder, Mazzini, and Ataturk; Kenyatta and Levesque; Ho Chi Minh and Gandhi? (Never mind that Gandhi shared Andrew Lytle's enthusiasm for spinning wheels.) Even without the Agrarians in it, what use is a category as diverse as that?

To be sure, nationalism does come in a great many flavors: if not as many as there are nations, still enough to be confusing. But Anthony Smith, a British student of nationalist ideology, argues that we can identify a "core doctrine" of nationalism common to all and distinct from the "supporting theories" that grow up around it.[5] Among the "themes that recur endlessly in the literature of nationalism," he finds "identity, purity, regeneration, the 'enemy,' historical roots, self-emancipation, building the 'new man' and the 'new community,' collective sover-eignty and participation." These themes provide the motive for "the peculiar activities of nationalist movements"—the "philological, an-thropological and historical researches of small coteries of intellec-tuals," for instance, or the "secret societies pressing for reform and independence." (Devotees of Agrarianism will know of the Vander-bilt secret society with the rather ominous name of "Phalanx," which chartered a branch at the Normal School in Murfreesboro, and then lapsed back into a secrecy so profound that it has not been heard of since.)

Smith writes also of the virtually universal Golden Age discovered in the nation's communal past, "a pristine state of true collective individuality," against which the present is measured and inevitably

5. The "supporting theories" may be romantic, liberal, theocratic, populist, lately even Marxist, and the nature of a nationalism's supporting theory is obvi-ously not inconsequential. I hope, some other time, to develop the observation that the Agrarians' "supporting theory" was unusual—an indigenous growth, as their frequent references to Calhoun suggest.

found wanting. But this Golden Age is not a strictly empirical description of past time; it is constructed to satisfy "present yearnings for an ideal community." Nationalism's envisioned future community "will not replicate that of the Golden Age, but it will recapture its spirit and set man free to be himself."

All nationalists search for "dignity" and for "roots," threatened or denied not by property relations and class antagonisms but by elements alien to the subjected nation. And, as Smith puts it: "The recovery of self-respect must be preceded by a return to 'nature'—'as in the days of old,' when the community mirrored the conditions of nature and produced 'natural men.'" But nationalism is not an uncritical traditionalism. On the contrary, it is "an attack on tradition and modernity alike, insofar as they obscure and distort the genuine relationship of man with nature and with his fellow-man." It is "a vision of the future which restores to man his 'essence,' his basic pattern of living and being, which was once his undisputed birthright."

I have quoted Smith at length because it seems to me that, as a description of what the Agrarians were up to, it would be hard to improve on this summary, written by a present-day British sociologist who has probably never heard of them. The point is that what has proved to be the lasting contribution of *I'll Take My Stand,* its vision of the good life, may be an immediate outgrowth of its authors' "sectionalism." The latter is not simply an accidental, and perhaps unfortunate, side issue. The Agrarians' myth of the South differs from other nationalist visions not in its general outlines or in the impulse that produced it, but in the raw materials its creators had to work with and the talent they brought to its making.

We can explore this analogy—parallel, model, call it what you will—a bit further.[6] Students of nationalism have offered a number of generalizations about their subject, and we can ask how well these apply to *I'll Take My Stand* and its authors. One of these generaliza-

---

6. A pleasant parlor game can be played by extracting passages from Nehru, Sun Yat Sen, Mazzini, or Herder, and matching them with equivalent passages from *I'll Take My Stand* and *Who Owns America?* An early draft of this essay went on and on in that fashion, but I have deleted most of that material in this version.

tions is that many of the characteristics of nationalist thought can be traced to the characteristics of nationalist thinkers. The early stages of nationalist movements, for instance, are almost always dominated by young, urban, literary intellectuals. By those attributes and usually by others as well, these leaders are both alienated from the culture they seek to defend and marginal, if that, to the existing structure of political power. The common emphases of nationalist thought stem from those dilemmas and (students of such movements argue) are attempts to resolve them.[7]

Consider, for instance, the link between nationalism and youth, a linkage evident even in the names of many movements: Young Italy, Young Ireland, Young Egypt, Young China, the Young Czechs, and the Young Turks. Although nationalists may grow old, few old people become nationalists. The task, after all, is to rejuvenate a culture (and the young are also unlikely to have much stake in the existing settlement). The Twelve Southerners were no different; indeed, one reviewer of *I'll Take My Stand* mocked them as "the young Confederates." One often forgets (at least I often forget) just how young they were. At the time of the Monkey Trial, their average age was thirty. Ransom, sometimes regarded as the movement's elder statesman, was thirty-five. When the book appeared, several of the contributors were still in their twenties. (And consider Phalanx: student societies are an almost universal accompaniment to nationalism.)

The theme of generational conflict is present in most nationalisms, at least in their early stages (until, we may suppose, some of the nationalists have time to age). The introductory statement to *I'll Take My Stand* calls on "the younger Southerners" to "come back to the support of the Southern tradition," and when Ransom appealed to "my own generation" to defend the South, he was still under forty. Nationalism's appeal to youth is often coupled with a rejection of old and traditional leadership, except for those leaders conveniently dead.

---

7. Perhaps I should point out that, like any reductionist explanation of an ideology, this one does not address itself to the ideology's truth or justice; rather, it seeks to explain why that position is held by one group rather than another, and in a particular situation.

I do not believe that *I'll Take My Stand* presents *any* living Southerner as admirable, except for "William Remington," Henry Blue Kline's alter ego. Even the estimable Cousin Lucius—as Wade's sketch says, "Mas' Lucius done dead!"

No, nationalists everywhere scorn those who, like most of us over thirty, have made their peace with oppression—which may put a new light on Ransom's contemptuous dismissal of "inept Southern politicians." And the well-known crack about the Fugitives' being in flight from "the high-caste Brahmins of the Old South" can be matched with the remarks of Indian nationalists who were "fleeing" *real* Brahmins.

The same scorn is directed at those fellow nationals of any generation who fail to see the self-evident rightness of the nationalist analysis (and there are always many who do not see it, especially at first). One of the great appeals of nationalism is that, like all powerful modern ideologies, it can explain everything, including its own setbacks. So if Southern newspapers, almost without exception, greeted *I'll Take My Stand* with ridicule or alarm—well, it was about what Owsley expected from organs "largely subsidized by Northern-owned power companies and Wall-Street-owned banks." And those Southern intellectuals who were hostile to the Agrarians were, after all, "fawning for the favor of these [same] corporations or of other powerful Northern groups." Lytle also denounced the "modern scalawags who . . . openly acknowledge their servile dependence on New York" and "consciously or unconsciously" serve the interests of Northern industry "for a small share of the booty." Almost identical passages could be multiplied endlessly from the literature of other nationalist groups.

Explaining rejection by the "folk" themselves is trickier. (Marxists, of course, have a similar problem.) Nationalists often argue that their nation has been degraded by its situation to the point where it cannot respond. We find similar themes in *I'll Take My Stand*. Stark Young, for instance, argued that Southerners had been disoriented by modernity, "by the World War and its aftermath; the churches, trying to keep up with the times . . . ; the schools; the moving pictures; and, most of all, the press." He wrote of his friend, a doctor, who was "confused, like a child watching the train passing." Sometimes this line almost expresses contempt for the people one is trying to speak for. Nationalists have such high expectations for their people that they are often disappointed, and some wind up like Clemenceau, who (it is said) loved France but rather disliked Frenchmen. Among the Agrarians, Kline was probably least sympathetic with the "apathetic mass," "bovine-passive," but Ransom also had some hard things to say about "broken-down Southerners." It may be just as well for the Agrarians that so few ordinary Southerners read their defense of the Southern tradition.

The Agrarians themselves were not ordinary young Southerners, and they knew it. Nationalists have nowhere been ordinary young people. The early stages of nationalist movements everywhere attract literary folk, which accounts for the emphasis Smith observes on cultural issues like roots, and history, and national dignity. Nationalism is the original single-issue politics, and its tendency to subordinate other issues accounts for the frequent difficulty of classifying it as politically left or right. The founders of nationalist movements (unlike the economists, engineers, and soldiers who often take over later on) are usually interested in political economy primarily as it impinges on cultural identity and what the Scottish Nationalists call "national self-respect." As an SNP tract I once saw put it: "When the Scottish political renaissance has taken us to independence once again, then will be the time to take up left, right, or centre views."

When nationalists come from a nation that is "peripheral" in the world economy, one like the South of the 1920s that produces raw materials and supplies unskilled labor for a more "advanced" economy, they often adopt the same stance the Agrarians did, rejecting the Western science and technology that, in any case, they do not have, and insisting that their very backwardness in Western terms has preserved a spiritual and cultural superiority. From the nineteenth-century Slavophils to the Hindu nationalists of early twentieth-century India to the apostles of negritude today, we often find Westernized intellectuals assuring the masses of peripheral nations of their superiority to those who dominate them economically and threaten to do so culturally.

And we can often observe the very same division that existed among the Agrarians between the "fundamentalists" (as Owsley called them) who wish to arrest industrialization altogether, and those (among whom Owsley put himself) who wish to domesticate industrialism and assimilate it to their valued culture. To be sure, some nationalists positively lust to industrialize their nations, but their motive is often to win international respect and to bolster national self-respect. This motive was not entirely alien to at least one of the Twelve Southerners: when Owsley proposed his program of reform, he remarked that "with such political economy, the South would soon become one of the most important parts of the world."

And the Agrarians' emphasis on education and propaganda was absolutely typical of nationalist movements. Their complaints about Southern schoolchildren singing "Land of the Pilgrims' Pride" read like nothing so much as the complaints of Algerians forced to read about "our ancestors, the Gauls," or Indians raised on "our Anglo-Saxon heritage." Nothing is more annoying than having someone else tell you who you are. Control of education and the media—thus, control of *mythology*—is probably the first nationalist issue.

Another characteristic of nationalists is that they tend to come from precisely the least traditional elements of the nation. Their educations, their occupations, their travels, and their location in cities distance them from the culture they propose to defend. Moreover, they often *begin* at some distance from it; it is almost a commonplace that nationalists are likely to be from the geographical fringes of their nation, and they are often from minority groups as well.[8] Given the Agrarians' Vanderbilt setting, perhaps we should not make too much of the fact that most of the twelve were Kentuckians and Tennesseans, men of the upper and western South. But although Tate's mother allowed him to believe that he had been born in the Old Dominion until he was thirty, the shameful fact is that there were no Virginians or South Carolinians in the group, no one from what the

---

8. I collect examples but will content myself here with two: the Ayatollah Khomeini, who grew up on Iran's border with India, and the one whom the Romans crucified as "King of the Jews," who came from the first-century Palestinian equivalent of East Tennessee, as Nathanael reminds us in John 1:46.

residents of those states believe to be the spiritual heart of the Old South. In fact, there were very few (only three, I believe) from the Deep South, the old plantation belt that set the political tone of the South after Reconstruction.

It may be, in other words, that most of the Agrarians were *born* at some distance, geographically and psychologically, from the dominant tradition of the South. Certainly, as I have mentioned, their view of the South's tradition differed in its emphasis from the prevailing view a couple of hundred miles south of Nashville. It was a Georgian, after all, U. B. Phillips, who insisted that "the central theme of Southern history and the cardinal test of a Southerner" was unwavering commitment to white supremacy.

It appears that someone has to stand at a certain remove from his culture in order to see it as something that can be dealt with, accepted or rejected by an act of the will, analyzed and *used.* And the Agrarians shared another experience that contributed to that distancing, one that has produced nationalists elsewhere, namely, the experience of having lived outside their native culture. "Exile is the nursery of nationalism," Lord Acton observed, "as oppression is the school of liberalism," and I believe that all of the twelve had lived outside the South before *I'll Take My Stand* was written.

The young provincial in the metropolis is a stock figure in many countries, and the experience does not even usually produce a nationalist. But when the provinces stand in a colonial or semicolonial relation to the metropolis, when they have a distinct culture, when the provincial meets with rebuff or condescension, when he has the sensibility and the education to think about these matters ideologically— well, then the metropolis is asking for trouble.

A student or professional may have removed himself from the provinces precisely in order to succeed, on the terms of the metropolitan culture. If he fails (or if he succeeds, but is not allowed to forget his origins). . . . The biographies of nationalists often reveal that they rejected the dominant culture only after it rejected them. Those who have seen the photographs of Gandhi decked out as an English solicitor will perhaps understand what I mean.

There are other ways being away from home breeds nationalism besides reminding expatriates that they come from a culture viewed as inferior. In some part, we may see simply the politicization of home-sickness. Michael Collins, an Irish nationalist, once tried to explain what he stood for: "Once, years ago, a crowd of us were going along the Shepherd's Bush Road [in London] when out of a lane came a chap with a donkey—just the sort of donkey and just the sort of cart that they have at home. He came out quite suddenly and quite abruptly and we all cheered him. No one who has not been an exile will understand me, but I stand for that." In *I'll Take My Stand,* Stark Young wrote from New York of the sort of experience that "brings tears to your eyes because of its memory of some place." "That place," he said, "is your country."

Being among people whose ways are different makes you aware of the ways you have left. Owsley learned a great deal at the University of Chicago that was not in the curriculum: some thirty years after *I'll Take My Stand* he still remembered what he had experienced as the absence of "the common courtesies of life." Kline also wrote of this experience: "William Remington" returned to the South to find "people living more nearly by his values and sensing life with sympathies closer to his own." And Ransom congratulated Tate in 1927 on his "stubbornness of temperament and habit," observing that he knew a great many like Tate, "born and bred in the South who go North and cannot bring themselves to surrender to an alien mode of life."

Finally, leaving home can make some things seem unimportant. Ernest Renan remarked in a famous essay on nationalism that the existence of a nation requires that a great many things be forgotten: in particular, those things that divide the nation. It is easier in London than on the Indian subcontinent to forget the history of mutual distrust between Hindu and Muslim, and African tribal differences may look insignificant from Paris, if not within the new African states themselves. Just so, from New York, Paris, or Oxford, yeoman and planter may have looked much alike, or at least their similarity may have seemed more important than the differences that were pretty much what Southern politics was all about. (There is no evidence of it in *I'll Take My Stand,* but later some Southern expatriates—Robert Penn Warren, for one—have come to realize how much black and white Southerners have in common.)

All of this is by way of saying that, for cultural nationalists, their tradition is not something that is second nature. Their experiences have left them like beached fish aware for the first time of water. Their acceptance of tradition, their nationality itself, must be willed. In Tate's marvelously ambiguous phrase, they must take hold of their tradition "by violence."

Elie Kedourie is the student of nationalism who has put the matter in its starkest form. Modernization, he says, gives some young people the experiences and education to see their culture from "outside," as it were; it half-alienates them from that culture. At the same time, it provides them with the ideological vocabulary to interpret their alienation and to defend their culture, and modernization is itself what they protest. This alienation, this partial uprooting, is the motif that unites all of the generalizations about nationalist leaders. It is also conspicuously characteristic of most of the twelve Agrarians, as the North Carolina–born University of Chicago philosopher Richard Weaver pointed out in his essay "Agrarianism in Exile" some time ago. I will not belabor the point, but allow me simply to illustrate it, in the words of perhaps the least "modern" of the twelve, Donald Davidson.

In a lovely essay on Sacred Harp singing, Davidson came close to implying that the unexamined culture is the only one worth living in. Here is his description of the unself-conscious relation of the people of "Eden" to their culture: "The folks of Eden do not have to study much over what to keep and what to abandon, because they know how they wish to live. . . . Indeed, they do not particularly notice what they are keeping or make any great outcry pro and con." Compare that to Davidson's own attitude, expressed elsewhere: "We must recover the past, or at least in some way realize it in order that we may bring the most genuine and essential parts of our tradition forward in contact with the inevitable new tradition now in the process of formation." No Edenite could write that. Only someone who has been driven from the garden has the distance to treat its culture analytically, to speak of "parts of our tradition."

I have indicated how that distancing can come about, and a number of scholars have written about it, but few so well as Davidson, who could turn a nice bit of sociology himself when he put his hand to it. He wrote once of the "moment of self-consciousness" that comes when a traditional society first faces modernization: "The invasion seems always to force certain individuals into an examination of their total inheritance that perhaps they would not otherwise have undertaken. . . . Their glance is always retrospective, but their point of view is thoroughly contemporary." The moment of self-consciousness is "the moment when a writer awakes to realize what he and his people truly are, in comparison with what they are being urged to become." Davidson was arguing that these conditions produce great literature, as in Ireland, Russia, and the South, but students of politics observe that they also produce nationalist movements.

And sometimes the nationalist and the artist are one and the same. When that is the case, what are intended to be tracts and manifestoes can speak to issues more important and more enduring than the ethnic or regional conflict that occasions them. *I'll Take My Stand* is such a volume. If it had been only a sectionalist broadside, it would not have the continuing, even increasing, importance it does appear to have.

Indeed, it would have very little importance of any sort, even historical, because as nationalist agitators the Agrarians were simply not very effective. As the 1930s passed, they gained a few converts and rather more fellow travelers, but many of the original twelve fell away—or perhaps "moved on" is the better phrase. In the essay I have mentioned, Richard Weaver, one of those fellow travelers, had some wise observations about why. As Weaver recognized, the parallels to other nationalist movements can be found there, as well. By the time of World War II, Agrarianism as a sectionalist movement was ailing, and it seems to me that the war and the fifteen years that followed, which emphasized American unity and American destiny—*American* nationalism—finished off the specifically Southern aspects of the Agrarian protest. The same twenty years also completed the South's transformation into an urban and industrial society, and cut the ground from under anyone who sought to identify the Southern way of life with agrarianism.

Let me close, though, by observing one more common feature of nationalist movements, a feature that may have some lessons for us.

We can see, from outside or in retrospect, that the national tradition that nationalists take hold of is always selective, and sometimes selective to the point of distortion. The tendency is to oversimplify, to identify the nation with one aspect of its culture and to see everything else, wrongly, as dependent on that one aspect: the Russian church, the Chinese family, the German language, perhaps even the Southern farmer.

But the reality is always more complex than an ideology can comprehend, and nations are more resilient things than most of their defenders acknowledge—as the Russian, Chinese, and German experiences in their different ways have shown us. George Orwell had some insightful things to say about nationalism, and about nations. He wrote once that it takes some very great disaster to destroy a national culture. In England, he said, "the Stock Exchange will be pulled down, the horse plough will give way to the tractor, the country houses will be turned into children's holiday camps, the Eton and Harrow match will be forgotten, but England will still be England, an everlasting animal stretching into the future and the past, and, like all living things, having the power to change out of recognition and yet remain the same."

I'll Take My Stand closed with some very similar thoughts about the South, Stark Young's observation that "the South changing must be the South still." I hope it is appropriate for one who shares the Agrarians' affection for the South to endorse those thoughts, and to close his essay with the hope that what Orwell said of England may be so for the South.

Continuities and Change

The Incredible Shrinking South

with James M. Kohls and Carol Hanchette

In a 1976 *Social Forces* article, I demonstrated a technique for mapping "folk" or "vernacular" regions, using the incidence of regional terms in the names of businesses and associations listed in metropolitan telephone directories. Essentially the technique defines a region as that part of a nation where nonresidential directory listings are likely to begin with a regional identifier. The article mapped both "the South," defined by listings beginning with *Southern,* and "Dixie," defined by the incidence of that word, using telephone directories from the early 1970s.

Ideally, we should examine regionally identified listings as a percentage of all nonresidential listings, but I took the shortcut of mapping regional listings as a fraction of listings beginning with the term *American* on the assumption that the latter is proportional to total nonresidential listings. (The results suggested that this assumption was approximately correct.) A computer mapping program was used to interpolate values of the resulting statistics S (*Southern* entries divided by *American* entries) and D (*Dixie* entries divided by *American* entries) for areas between the metropolitan data points. In general the results coincided with regional definitions derived from quite different criteria, which suggested that the technique was valid and reliable.[1]

The two regions, the South and Dixie, were not quite the same, but

1. Wilbur Zelinsky subsequently adapted the technique and applied it to the definition of other major regions of the United States.

the differences made sense. Using *Dixie* in a business name, like sing-ing the song or flying the Confederate flag, indicates attachment to a historic symbol of the South, but *Southern* can serve simply as a loca-tor, like *southeastern,* a label for an enterprise that is, or aspires to be, regional in scope. *Dixie,* in other words, is a relatively pure measure of sectional identification, usually connoting a shared history of excep-tionalism and opposition to the rest of the country; *Southern* can have the same connotations, but it can also indicate merely integration into the South's developing economy. Both conceptually and (as it turned out) geographically, *Dixie* evoked the Old South of plantation agricul-ture, *Southern* the New South of commerce and industry.

Time for a Reexamination

Since the early 1970s, a number of changes have taken place that should have affected how Southerners think of their region and, possibly, how they refer to it. Consequently, it ought to be worthwhile to look again at the South and at Dixie, defined in these terms.

For several reasons, it seems likely that the word *Dixie* is losing some of its currency. In the first place, race relations in the South, the principal component of Southern exceptionalism and the principal cause of white Southern defensiveness in the recent past, have im-proved, to the point where it is now possible to argue seriously that they are at least as good as those elsewhere, if not actually better. In addition, the election in 1976 of the first undeniably Southern presi-dent since Andrew Johnson may have undermined white Southerners' historic feelings of exclusion and powerlessness. The white South's traditional symbols of defiance may simply have less appeal now than they did even in the recent past.

Moreover, for obvious reasons, black Southerners are not partic-ularly attached to those symbols. To the extent that Southern blacks are now fully citizens or customers whose opinions must be taken into account, those who name businesses might well choose to avoid the word *Dixie* in deference to their feelings. Similarly, in parts of the South where large numbers of migrants from outside the South have settled—that is, in many of the region's major cities—*Dixie* in a business name might be as likely to repel customers as to attract them. For all of these reasons, it would not be surprising to find that use of *Dixie* is less widespread than it was as recently as fifteen or twenty years ago.

It is harder to say what should be happening to *Southern*. The same developments affecting the use of *Dixie* should be affecting that of *Southern*, and James Shortridge has presented data to suggest that many residents of Virginia and North Carolina now think of themselves as Easterners rather than as Southerners. On the other hand, the South's economic development has continued; although the image of a prosperous Sun Belt may be misleading, the region is certainly no longer the nation's number one economic problem (as Franklin Roosevelt called it). This development may be encouraging the growth of regionwide businesses and, thus, possibly the use of *Southern* in business names. In other words, Southern businesses—some of them perhaps named that—have proliferated.

We consulted telephone directories for all but one of the cities examined in the earlier study (Lincoln, Nebraska, was not readily available) for years between 1985 and 1988. In each case, the same data were collected as in the early 1970s, the same two ratios were computed, and the same computer program was used to interpolate from the data points.

The Shrinking South

Table 1 shows the values of S from the 1976 article and for the later period (labeled 1988). In general, the picture is one more of continuity than of change. The core area of the South, measured this way, is still to be found where it was before, in the conventionally defined Deep South states of Georgia, Alabama, and Mississippi, with relatively high values also to be found in Louisiana, Tennessee, North and South Carolina, and lower but still appreciable values in Virginia, Florida, Arkansas, Kentucky, and eastern parts of Texas.

Some differences can be found in detail, however. It seems fair to say that the past fifteen years have seen something of a "consolidation" of the South. Values of S have remained roughly the same, or even increased, in the Southern heartland while decreasing in border areas.

Table 1.   Ratio of Southern to American Entries (S), Ratio of Dixie to American Entries (D), and Number of American Entries, 1976 and 1988, by City.

State/City	S 1976	S 1988	D 1976	D 1988	American Entries 1976	American Entries 1988
Alabama						
Birmingham	.86	1.22	.58	.16	146	207
Montgomery	.98	.89	.55	.21	49	90
Mobile	1.02	1.01	.34	.19	58	99
Mississippi						
Jackson	.86	1.22	.51	.42	69	90
Biloxi-Gulfport	.96	1.42	.70	.37	27	38
Georgia						
Atlanta	.70	.71	.22	.15	450	831
Columbus	.73	1.55	.49	.48	37	31
Savannah	.91	1.31	.50	.40	34	48
Augusta	1.11	1.02	.63	.32	36	62
Macon	1.16	1.11	.84	.43	31	44
Louisiana						
New Orleans	.70	.77	.33	.26	235	283
Baton Rouge	.95	.70	.22	.14	46	131
Shreveport	1.08	.92	.27	.18	66	118
Tennessee						
Nashville	.76	.65	.28	.17	144	217
Knoxville	.81	.62	.36	.23	67	104
Memphis	.86	.65	.42	.15	151	237
Chattanooga	.90	.96	.48	.31	67	85
South Carolina						
Charleston	.60	.69	.36	.18	50	91
Columbia	.68	1.01	.35	.30	77	98
Greenville	.86	.60	.39	.31	70	114
North Carolina						
Asheville	.70	.59	.14	.03	47	39
Charlotte	.72	.68	.36	.17	130	204
Raleigh	.74	.81	.19	.14	57	111
Durham	.76	.97	.20	.08	25	36
Winston-Salem	.84	.81	.43	.30	37	53
Fayetteville	.93	.54	.56	.14	27	50
Greensboro	.97	.76	.33	.12	64	105
Florida						
St. Petersburg	.45	.34	.17	.07	75	137
West Palm Beach	.45	.40	.33	.19	87	178
Orlando	.47	.42	.18	.08	139	330
Fort Lauderdale	.49	.36	.11	.10	148	317

State/City	S 1976	1988	D 1976	1988	American Entries 1976	1988
Florida (continued)						
Miami	.60	.32	.28	.10	257	699
Jacksonville	.67	.60	.36	.16	132	201
Tampa	.69	.42	.28	.12	94	224
Pensacola	.74	.82	.38	.16	39	87
Tallahassee	.89	1.32	.26	.26	27	34
Virginia						
Roanoke	.35	.42	.22	.24	55	62
Norfolk	.46	.31	.13	.07	111	194
Richmond	.53	.56	.15	.07	130	192
Kentucky						
Lexington	.45	.35	.29	.08	56	88
Louisville	.46	.33	.37	.32	138	151
Arkansas						
Little Rock	.53	.33	.20	.09	83	160
Texas						
El Paso	.04	.04	.00	.00	81	118
Amarillo	.10	.04	.00	.00	41	76
Abilene	.10	.12	.03	.06	39	52
Dallas	.19	.20	.04	.02	477	888
San Antonio	.21	.15	.04	.04	165	298
Austin	.23	.14	.03	.01	76	269
Corpus Christi	.26	.27	.04	.04	65	105
Fort Worth	.27	.16	.03	.03	122	372
Houston	.36	.27	.13	.07	419	820
Port Arthur	.42	.38	.08	.00	24	21
Galveston	.53	.34	.07	.09	30	32
Oklahoma						
Oklahoma City	.16	.09	.01	.01	208	292
Tulsa	.38	.13	.06	.01	127	245
Delaware/Maryland/D.C.						
Washington	.08	.04	.01	.00	680	961
Wilmington	.13	.06	.00	.00	63	119
Dover	.13	.13	.02	.01	45	69
Baltimore	.21	.07	.05	.03	346	472
West Virginia/Ohio						
Wheeling	.00	.00	.00	.00	32	30
Cleveland	.04	.01	.01	.00	387	420
Columbus	.06	.05	.03	.02	199	253

Table 1. Ratio of Southern to American Entries (S), Ratio of Dixie to American Entries (D), and Number of American Entries, 1976 and 1988, by City (continued).

	S		D		American Entries	
State/City	1976	1988	1976	1988	1976	1988
West Virginia/Ohio (continued)						
Dayton	.11	.03	.18	.12	105	152
Cincinnati	.12	.05	.23	.12	212	257
Huntington	.24	.21	.05	.00	21	29
Indiana/Illinois						
Peoria	.02	.00	.02	.02	51	55
Chicago	.03	.02	.03	.01	1153	1035
Indianapolis	.11	.05	.01	.02	210	311
Springfield (Ill.)	.15	.00	.00	.00	46	68
Evansville	.30	.06	.02	.00	40	66
Missouri/Kansas						
Kan. City (Mo.)	.06	.03	.03	.01	320	400
St. Louis	.12	.08	.02	.00	379	430
Topeka	.13	.03	.03	.00	32	69
Miscellaneous						
Duluth	.00	.03	.00	.00	31	36
Boise	.00	.00	.00	.01	33	85
Grand Rapids	.00	.00	.01	.00	80	139
Sioux Falls	.00	.00	.04	.03	28	40
Scranton	.00	.02	.04	.00	69	53
Salt Lake City	.01	.00	.00	.00	180	249
Colorado Springs	.02	.00	.00	.00	58	134
Boston	.02	.01	.00	.00	376	396
Albuquerque	.02	.01	.01	.01	128	174
Buffalo	.02	.04	.01	.00	156	151
St. Paul	.02	.03	.01	.01	170	148
Portland	.02	.01	.01	.00	227	260
Minneapolis	.02	.02	.01	.00	325	394
Des Moines	.02	.04	.02	.00	88	119
Omaha	.02	.01	.02	.01	132	177
Spokane	.03	.02	.00	.00	61	103
Newark	.03	.01	.01	.01	182	163
San Francisco	.03	.02	.01	.00	416	461
Detroit	.03	.03	.02	.01	475	339
Las Vegas	.03	.02	.05	.06	59	54
Philadelphia	.04	.03	.00	.00	502	430
Camden	.04	.01	.01	.01	118	171
Pittsburgh	.05	.03	.00	.01	283	314
Los Angeles	.05	.01	.02	.01	914	974
Rochester	.05	.02	.04	.02	95	101
Phoenix	.06	.03	.01	.00	205	578

Consider:

> In the early 1970s, seven Midwestern cities had S values over .10: Cincinnati and Dayton, Ohio; Evansville and Indianapolis, Indiana; Springfield, Illinois; St. Louis, Missouri; and Topeka, Kansas. For every one of those cities the S value dropped below .10 during the roughly fifteen years in question.
>
> In the same period, nine of the eleven data points in Maryland, Delaware, the District of Columbia, West Virginia, Kentucky, Arkansas, and Oklahoma showed decreases; the other two were unchanged—and one of them was Wheeling, which had an S score of zero at both times.
>
> In Texas, S values decreased at seven of the eleven data points, increased at three, and were unchanged at one. The increases, however, were negligible; some of the decreases were substantial—for instance, those at Houston and Galveston.
>
> In Florida, S values increased only at the two data points in northern Florida, Pensacola and Tallahassee, while decreasing at all of the seven points elsewhere in the state.
>
> By contrast, in the Southern core area, values of S tended to increase. Nine of the thirteen cities in Mississippi, Alabama, Georgia, and South Carolina showed increases; the seven cities with increases greater than .30 were Jackson and Biloxi-Gulfport, Mississippi; Birmingham, Alabama; Columbus and Savannah, Georgia; Columbia, South Carolina; and Tallahassee, Florida.

When the new values of S are mapped, the result is an apparent shrinkage of the region. Whatever value is chosen to mark "the border" of the South, the region it defines is more compact than it was fifteen years earlier.

Figure 1, for example, shows the contour lines at S = .10 for the two periods. In the original article, this value was taken to indicate the South's "sphere of influence," extending into the lower Midwest and the historic border states. By the late 1980s, that Greater South had receded somewhat, retreating from the Mason-Dixon Line, pulling back toward the Ohio River.

Figure 2 shows the isopleth that seemed in the early 1970s perhaps the best single choice for a boundary line, if a single one had

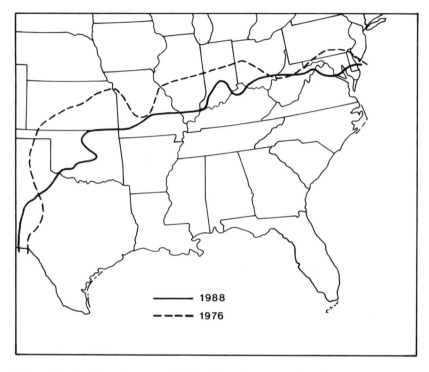

Figure 1. *Southern* 10 percent of *American* (S = .10), 1976 and 1988.

to be chosen (S = .35). It enclosed essentially the ten easternmost Confederate states plus Kentucky and the eastern parts of Oklahoma and Texas. Fifteen years later, that boundary had receded from northern Virginia and Kentucky, from Oklahoma altogether, and—thanks to the diminished value for Little Rock—from a large part of Arkansas.

Interestingly, the southernmost part of the South, southern Florida, has now also dropped out of the South by this reckoning. Figure 3 sheds further light on this phenomenon. In the early 1970s, most of Florida was part of the core South, defined by S values of .60 or greater, but there were exceptions in the southeast and west central parts of the state. Now the exceptions have become the rule: no part of peninsular Florida is any longer included in the Southern heartland. Figure 3 also shows erosion in Virginia and the Carolinas and in Arkansas and east Texas.

If the measurement premise is accepted, these data indicate a

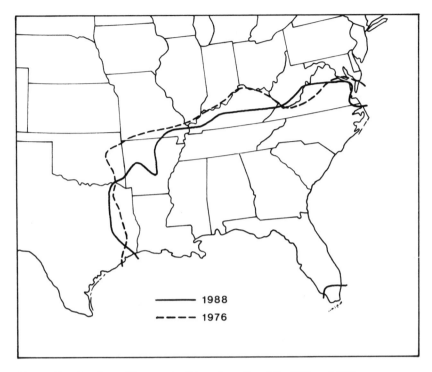

Figure 2. *Southern* 35 percent of *American* (S = .35), 1976 and 1988.

waning of regional identification or integration (at least relative to national identification or integration) on the borders of the historic South. In nearly every case, however, what is decreasing is the ratio of *Southern* to *American* entries, not the absolute number of *Southern* entries. Usually, there are more *Southern* entries than there were before; they have just not increased as rapidly as *American* entries— or, by assumption, as the total number of nonresidential entries.

Disappearing Dixie

In the case of *Dixie,* however, the absolute number of such entries has decreased in most cities, strikingly so in some cases. The statistic D increased in only five of the cities and not appreciably in them (the largest increase was from .03 to .06 in Abilene). For whatever reason, the word *Dixie* appears to be going out of style—rapidly, in many parts of the South.

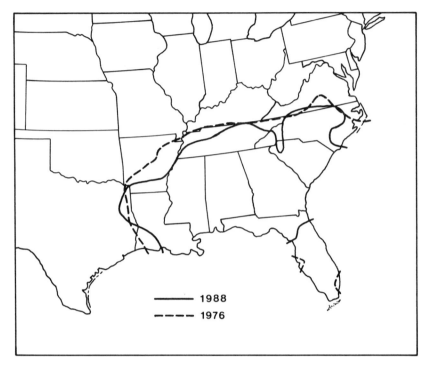

Figure 3. *Southern* 60 percent of *American* (S = .60), 1976 and 1988.

Although the contour for D = .06 (about the smallest value distinguishable above the "noise") is roughly the same for 1988 as for the earlier period, even it shows some attrition (Figure 4). In most border areas—northern and eastern Virginia, West Virginia, the lower Midwest, the Arkansas-Oklahoma border area, and East Texas—the .06 line is farther south and/or east than it was fifteen years earlier.

The pattern is more striking for the contour at D = .15. By 1988, the Appalachian secession from Dixie was even more pronounced than in the early 1970s, and Appalachia has been joined by most of Virginia, large parts of North Carolina, all of peninsular Florida, most of the Southwest, and Atlanta (Figure 5). Dixie, by this measure, has been reduced to northern Louisiana, the Deep South states from Mississippi to South Carolina, and northern Florida. Only parts of Tennessee, Kentucky, Virginia, and North Carolina—nearly all part of Dixie in the 1970s—are still included.

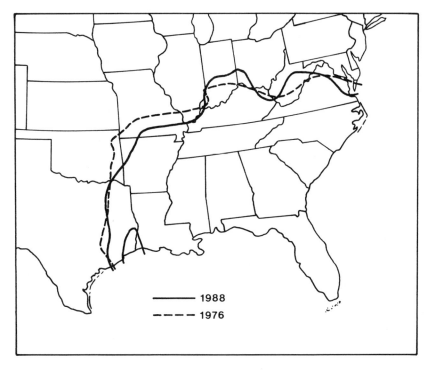

1988
1976

Figure 4.   *Dixie* 6 percent of *American* (D = .06), 1976 and 1988.

If we take a more demanding criterion, D = .25, Dixie simply dis-
solves as a coherent region (Figure 6). By the early 1970s, Atlanta,
most of Virginia, the Southwest, Appalachia, parts of North Carolina,
and most of peninsular Florida had already dropped out of Dixie;
however, the mapping program could still produce a region consist-
ing of the Deep South states from South Carolina to Mississippi, plus
Tennessee and Kentucky, and parts of some adjoining Southern states.
Fifteen years later, Dixie has been reduced to Mississippi, Georgia
outside Atlanta, up-country South Carolina, and an occasional iso-
lated city elsewhere—Chattanooga, Winston-Salem, Louisville, and
a couple of others. The most startling recent dropouts are the three
data points in Alabama, still "The Heart of Dixie" on its license plates
but no longer in its cities' telephone books. The most extreme example is Birmingham: while that city's *Southern* entries more than dou-
bled, its *Dixie* entries were reduced by more than half. In the early

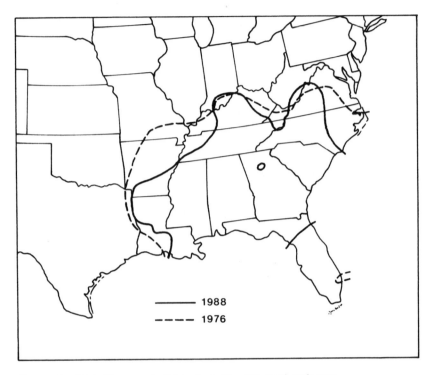

Figure 5.   *Dixie* 15 percent of *American* (D = .15), 1976 and 1988.

1970s, there were three *Southern* entries for every two *Dixie*s in Birmingham's directory; by the late 1980s, there were fifteen.

Summary and Conclusions

It appears that the South is being consolidated with sharper distinctions between the regional core and the surrounding periphery (Figure 7). At the core, we often find greater regional integration and identification now than fifteen years ago; elsewhere, we usually find less. In the Southern heartland, "Southern" businesses and associations are often increasing at a rate greater than "American" enterprises; elsewhere, *Southern* entries may be increasing, but more slowly than *American* ones, thus probably more slowly than business activity in general. We can speculate that areas part of the developing

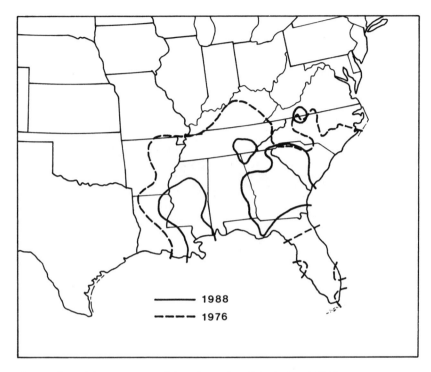

Figure 6. *Dixie* 25 percent of *American* (D = .25), 1976 and 1988.

Southern regional economy have increasing S ratios, but where Southern identification relies on sentiment alone, it may well be waning.

Certainly *Dixie,* a measure of that sentiment, seems to be dropping out of use (Figure 8). We speculated that the decrease—which is absolute, not just relative to *American* entries—reflects the waning of sectional feeling among Southern whites as well as economic activity by and deference to the feelings of Southern blacks and migrant whites. This suggests a limitation of the data we are using to examine this question. By necessity, all of the data come from urban areas, most of them fairly large cities. Southern cities are, in fact, where migrants are settling, where black economic and political power is concentrated, and where native whites are most assimilated to national (i.e., non-Southern) patterns. Between 1980 and 1985, for example, 90 percent of the new jobs in the South were created in Texas, Florida, and a dozen metropolitan areas elsewhere—all of them data points for this study.

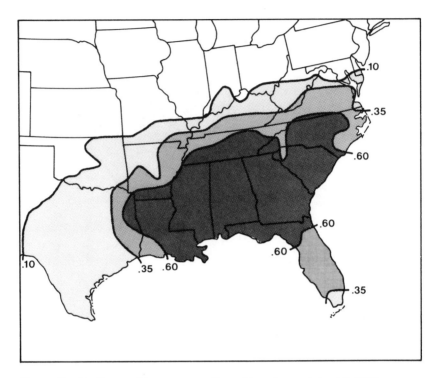

Figure 7. *Southern* entries as proportion of *American* entries (S), 1988.

The report of the 1986 Commission on the Future of the South, convened by the Southern Growth Policies Board, points to the emergence of two very different Souths: a metropolitan, urban, and suburban region that attracts migrants and offers middle-class standards of living to business and professional people; and a small-town and rural South, with stagnant or declining economies based on agriculture and low-wage, unskilled industrial jobs. Our data come disproportionately from the first of these Souths; we have filled in values for the small-town and rural South by simple extrapolation from the values for metropolitan areas.

Obviously, this may be misleading. There may also be two Souths when it comes to regional identification. Certainly the popularity of the songs of Hank Williams, Jr.—some of them with the word *Dixie* in the title—suggests that old-fashioned regional sentiment is flourishing somewhere, even if not in the names of urban and suburban businesses.

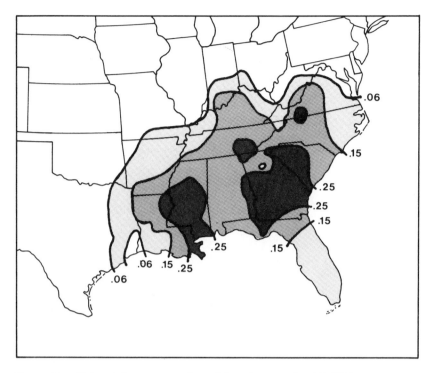

Figure 8. *Dixie* entries as proportion of *American* entries (D), 1988.

Lazy No More
Changing Regional Stereotypes

In 1933, in what has become a classic study of ethnic stereotyping, Daniel Katz and Kenneth Braley presented a group of Princeton undergraduates with a list of eighty-four adjectives and asked them to indicate which were "typical traits" of various racial, religious, and nationality groups, then which five were "most typical" of each group. (The groups were: Germans, English, Jews, Negroes, Turks, Japanese, Italians, Chinese, Americans, and Irish.) Their study has been replicated several times (for example, by G. M. Gilbert in 1951 and by Marvin Karlins and others in 1969), providing valuable data on ethnic stereotypes—at least those expressed by undergraduates.

In *The Enduring South,* I reported the results of a study Glen Elder and I conducted in 1970, in which we used the Katz and Braley adjective list to study the *regional* stereotypes held by a sample of white Southern undergraduates at the University of North Carolina at Chapel Hill—specifically, their images of "white Southerners" and "white Northerners." Despite the small sample size (forty-seven) and other limitations of the study, the results were quite clear.

In 1970, these students saw white Southerners as traditional or conservative, exemplifying a variety of "folk culture" traits ranging from familism to religiosity; as hospitable and polite; and as relatively lacking in ambition, energy, and industry. White Northerners were seen as roughly the opposite—hard-working, materialistic, intelligent, progressive—but also as loud and impolite. Perhaps surprisingly, these Southern students believed that many of these "Northern" characteristics were also typical *American* traits. No one was unwilling to describe regional groups, and regional stereotypes were well defined and widely shared; there was more agreement among the students in the sample about typical white Southern and white Northern traits than about, for instance, typical "Negro" traits.

These students' perceptions of regional differences were consistent with those of a national general population sample revealed in a 1957 Gallup Poll, and for that matter with the accounts of travelers and other observers dating back at least to the early nineteenth century. This consistency suggests that American regional imagery has been remarkably persistent and robust.

Nevertheless, many dramatic changes in American regions and regional relations since 1970 could have changed those images. In 1976, for instance, a conspicuously Southern president was elected, with much media attention (mostly admiring) to his regional origins. Ironically, four years later he was soundly defeated by a Californian supported by a substantial majority of white Southerners. The 1970s and 1980s witnessed the continuing diminution of regional economic and demographic differences, and many even began to speak of the emergence of a prosperous Sun Belt, said to include much of the historic South. Stepped-up migration to the metropolitan South presumably exposed more Southerners to actual interaction with non-Southern Americans (although the effects of such interaction on stereotypes may not be easy to predict). The same years also saw improvement in Southern race relations, at least as compared to those elsewhere.

In short, Americans, perhaps especially Southerners, have had much reason since 1970 to rethink their old ideas about the differences between North and South. With that in mind, I repeated the study in 1987. Fifty students at the University of North Carolina at Chapel Hill, self-identified as white Southerners on an attached personal data form, were given the Katz and Braley adjective list and asked to characterize three groups: "white Southerners," "white Northerners," and "Americans."[1] As in the earlier study, respondents were asked to check all of the eighty-four adjectives that were "typical" of each group, then to go back and circle the five "most typical."

In general, and allowing for sampling error, most of the same adjectives were used to describe the three groups in 1987 as in 1970. Figure 1, for example, shows what were seen as the "most typical" American traits in the two years.[2] (Those adjectives above the diagonal were chosen by a greater percentage of respondents in 1987 than in 1970; those below were chosen by a lower percentage.)

Materialistic was still the adjective most commonly applied to Americans (by 70 percent in 1970, 52 percent in 1987); *pleasure-loving, progressive,* and *ambitious* were also chosen by 20 percent or more in both years, and *individualistic, aggressive, ostentatious (showy), industrious, extremely nationalistic, imaginative,* and *scientifically-minded* were chosen by 10 percent or more both times. Seventy of the eighty-four adjectives were mentioned by fewer than 10 percent (most of them by none) in both years.[3]

Similarly, 20 percent or more of the respondents in both years chose *industrious, materialistic, progressive,* and *aggressive* as "most typical" traits of white Northerners (Figure 2). *Loud, ambitious, arrogant, rude, sophisticated, ostentatious (showy),* and *conceited* were chosen by 10 percent or more both times, and sixty-four of the eighty-four adjectives were consistently chosen by less than 10 percent.

In 1987, white Southerners' "most typical" traits still included *con-*

---

1. In the 1970 study subjects had also been asked for their perceptions of the several groups studied by Katz and Braley.

2. The raw data from the 1970 study were not retained, so the 1970 percentages for adjectives chosen by fewer than 8 percent of respondents have been arbitrarily set to 5 percent in Figures 1–3.

3. Adjectives chosen by fewer than 10 percent of respondents in both years (and thus not shown in Figures 1–3) were: *jovial, witty, superstitious, naive, revengeful, straightforward, stolid, happy-go-lucky, deceitful, efficient, persistent, radical, methodical, evasive, suspicious, shrewd, sly, meditative, stupid, unreliable, treacherous, cowardly, cruel, quarrelsome, gluttonous, pugnacious, suave, slovenly, reserved, quiet, ponderous, impulsive, suggestible, passionate, sensual, humorless, neat, imitative, frivolous, gregarious, musical, artistic, physically dirty, brilliant.*

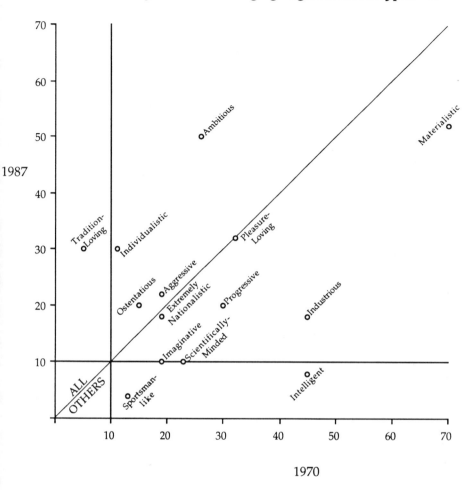

Figure 1. Percent choosing various adjectives as "most typical" of Americans, 1970 and 1987.

servative, tradition-loving, and courteous, all chosen by more than 20 percent in both years (Figure 3). Seven other characteristics—*loyal to family ties, conventional, stubborn, pleasure-loving, extremely nationalistic, generous,* and *faithful*—were chosen by more than 10 percent, and sixty-three by less than 10 percent, both times.

Obviously, in 1987 there was still considerable overlap between white Southern students' images of white Northerners and of Americans in general. Of the twelve characteristics attributed to Americans

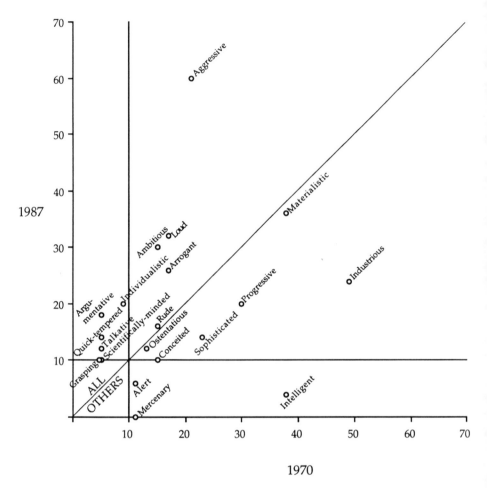

Figure 2.   Percent choosing various adjectives as "most typical" of white Northerners, 1970 and 1987.

by 10 percent or more of the respondents, eight were also attributed to white Northerners, only three—*pleasure-loving, extremely nationalistic,* and *tradition-loving*—to white Southerners. (*Imaginative* is an "American" trait attributed to neither regional group.)

Although the picture is primarily one of continuity, there were some changes. Statistically significant increases in the percentages calling Americans *tradition-loving* (from less than 8 percent to 30 percent) and *individualistic* (from 11 percent to 30 percent), and perhaps the

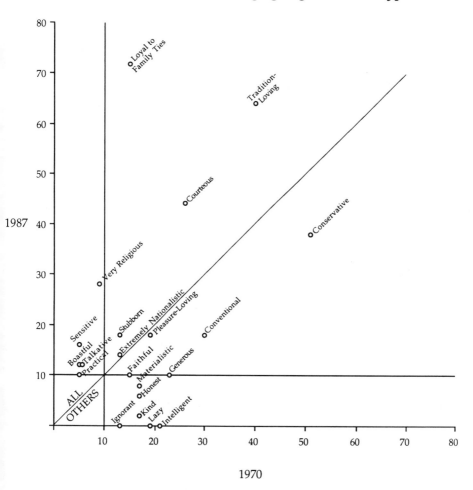

Figure 3. Percent choosing various adjectives as "most typical" of white Southerners, 1970 and 1987.

(smaller) decrease in the percentage calling them *progressive* as well, may reflect changes in the political climate between the end of the 1960s and the Reagan years.

In evaluating the effects of what was often said to be an acquisitive decade, a decrease for *materialistic* (from 70 to 52 percent) should be set beside an offsetting increase for *ambitious* (from 26 to 50 percent), and both adjectives can be instructively juxtaposed with the decrease for *industrious* (from 45 to 18 percent) and the precipitous decline for *intelligent* (from 45 to only 8 percent). Intelligence, like being *scientifically-minded,* is now far less likely to be regarded as a distinctively American trait.

As for perceptions of Northern and Southern traits, some of the differences reported in 1970 can be understood as attempts to explain the South's economic backwardness by reference to regional differences in character. By 1987, however, those attributions had decreased markedly. Like Americans in general, white Northerners were more likely to be seen as *ambitious* (up from 15 to 30 percent) but significantly less likely to be characterized as *intelligent* (down from 38 percent to 4 percent) or *industrious* (down from 49 percent to 24 percent). There were also smaller decreases in such "Northern" traits as *sophisticated, progressive,* and *alert.* White Southerners, too, were less likely than in 1970 to be seen as *intelligent* (down from 21 percent to zero), but respondents were also less likely to say that white Southerners are *lazy* or *ignorant* (down from 19 and 13 percent, respectively, to zero). We can speculate that the South's continuing economic development has improved Southerners' self-image in these respects. "Typical traits" that formerly distinguished prosperous Northerners from backward Southerners (similar to those that distinguished prosperous Americans from backward foreigners) are now a less prominent part of the picture.

Other stereotypical perceptions of regional differences, however, have become even more widespread than before. Although there was somewhat less agreement about typical American traits in 1987 than in 1970, consensus about typical traits of white Northerners and, especially, those of white Southerners actually increased.[4] It is point-

---

4. Katz and Braley suggested as a measure of the "definiteness" of a stereotype the minimum number of adjectives needed to capture half of the respondents' choices of "most typical" traits. Since each respondent chose five adjectives, total consensus would yield a score of 2.5. If respondents were in maximum possible disagreement (or if they chose at random), the choices would be evenly distributed across the eighty-four adjectives, for a score of 42. The index for "Americans" went from 6.1 to 8.1—that is, it took two more adjectives to capture half of the respondents' choices. The index for white Northerners, however, decreased slightly, from 8.6 to 8.0, and that for white Southerners fell from 9.2 to

less (though tempting) to try to explain all of these differences in detail, but I will at least mention most of them here.

For example, the decreasing proportions who say that white Southerners are *conservative* (down from 51 to 38 percent) or *conventional* (down from 30 to 18 percent) are offset by an increase in the percentage who call them *tradition-loving* (from 40 to 64 percent). It is hard to say what these changes might mean (they may reflect only slight changes in the connotations of the adjectives), but, by whatever name, this characteristic remains prominent in Southern students' image of their own regional group.

Other "Southern" traits also showed significant (and less ambiguous) increases. The increase for *very religious* (from 9 to 28 percent), for instance, may reflect the high visibility of Southern Evangelicals in the 1970s and 1980s. An especially striking increase was that for *loyal to family ties* (from 15 to 72 percent); by these students' reckoning, family loyalty is now the leading "most typical" trait of white Southerners.

The stereotypically Southern trait *courteous* also showed a substantial increase (from 26 to 44 percent), although declines for several other desirable traits—*generous* (from 23 to 10 percent), *kind* (from 17 to 2 percent), and *honest* (from 17 to 6 percent)—may suggest an interesting, emerging distinction between manners and character. In a related development, in 1987 significantly larger proportions of respondents identified as "Northern" such stereotypical traits as *loud* (17 percent to 32 percent), *argumentative* (from less than 8 percent to 18 percent), and especially *aggressive* (from 21 percent to 60 percent). There were also smaller increases for *quick-tempered* and *arrogant*— although not, interestingly, for *rude* (constant at 15–16 percent).

To repeat, however, aside from changes that may reflect increasing economic parity among the regions, the most striking result of this modest inquiry is the extent to which its results replicate those of the earlier study. White Southerners were no longer seen as lazy or ignorant, but white Northerners were still characterized (if decreas-

---

5.1. Half of all the choices made by these students, in other words, went to only five of the eighty-four adjectives: *loyal to family ties, tradition-loving, courteous, conservative,* and *very religious.*

ingly so) as industrious, progressive, and sophisticated. Moreover, the 1987 sample saw white Southerners as polite, if not actually benevolent, and as traditional, family-loving, and religious. These perceptions of white Southerners were present in 1970, but they were, if anything, even more widely held in 1987.

Too Good to Be False
An Essay in the Folklore of Social Science
with Gail Doss and Jeanne S. Hurlbert

No doubt many reading these words are familiar with the correlation between cotton prices and the lynching rate in the South. It sometimes seems that if social scientists know anything about lynching at all, they know that it increased when cotton prices fell and decreased when they rose. When we asked a sample of eighty-four members of the Society for the Psychological Study of Social Issues (SPSSI) what economic variable was associated with the lynching rate, thirty-three confidently replied that cotton prices were (another three more hesitantly mentioned "crops").[1]

Ever since this association was first reported in the social-psychological literature, it has served textbook writers and classroom teachers as a striking and memorable example to illustrate frustration-

1. Only nineteen acknowledged that they did not know: twenty-two speculated about variables like unemployment, income, and "depressed conditions," and seven took wild guesses (in one case, "the cost of beer"). The survey was conducted by postcard of a systematic sample of 100 from an alphabetical list of SPSSI members in 1970: eighty-four completed cards were returned. Sampling SPSSI members was a convenient way to reach social psychologists with a professional interest in social problems like lynching: they were presumably better informed on this topic than a cross section of other psychologists or sociologists would have been.

aggression theory. Undergraduates probably remember the example long after they have forgotten the concept it was meant to illustrate. Professional social psychologists, on the other hand, are likely to remember both example and concept; what they tend to forget (if they ever knew it) is the source of this finding. Not one of our respondents knew who *first* reported it, and only four knew that Carl I. Hovland and Robert R. Sears had introduced it to the social-psychology community, although ten more associated the finding with other researchers of the frustration-aggression school.

From one perspective, this collective amnesia is simply the ordinary operation of "normal science." Several decades after the research results were published, the findings have been assimilated into the common knowledge base; they are part of what "everybody knows," but they are seldom associated any longer with the names of the individual scientists who produced them. The image of science as a cumulative social enterprise—an edifice constructed by the labors of a multitude of humble worker bees operating within an established paradigm—encourages this view.

One could as easily say, however, that the story of cotton prices and lynching rates has entered the folklore of social psychology, that it has become a tale told by the elders around the campfires where the young are initiated into the tribe. This second view has much to recommend it: those SPSSI members who thought they recalled where they had heard of the correlation were nearly as likely to say that they had learned of it by word of mouth from teachers or colleagues as to say that they had seen a citation to the research, and much more likely to have done either of those than to believe they had read about it in the original source.[2]

Also lending its weight to a folkloric interpretation is the fact that the story has come to differ in some ways from the original, which was rather fabulous to begin with. The correlation of lynching rates

2. Eight could not recall where they had first heard of it; eleven said they had first heard about it from teachers or colleagues; eighteen recalled that they had learned about the research from citations to it; only four believed they had learned about the correlation from the original report. These categories were not mutually exclusive.

with cotton prices is something of a *myth,* in every sense of that word. Its history is an interesting one. There are some lessons in it for writers and researchers in the social sciences, lessons no less valuable for being old ones. More important, this story may also illustrate the operation of a structured impediment to reliable knowledge in social science.

Once Upon a Time . . .

In the early 1930s, in a book called *The Tragedy of Lynching,* Arthur F. Raper presented a graph of two statistics: the number of lynchings in "the nine cotton states" and the per-acre value of cotton for the years from 1901 to 1930 (omitting the "three abnormal [war] years," 1918–1920). (Raper wrote that the data had been assembled by T. J. Woofter, Jr. He did not say from where, but the lynching frequencies almost certainly came from the compilations by Monroe Work of Tuskegee Institute.) On the logarithmic scale of Raper's graph, lynchings showed an accelerating decrease for the period, and cotton prices per acre showed a slow, approximately linear increase.

Well aware of the fallacy of correlating trends per se (after all, most things either increase or decrease over three decades), Raper or his draftsman fitted trend lines to the curves, apparently free-hand. "It will be noted," Raper wrote, "that as a rule whenever the per acre value of cotton is above its trend the number of lynchings is below its trend. In other words, periods of relative prosperity bring reduction in lynching and periods of depression cause an increase." He added, "This relationship is shown by the correlation of –.532." Correlation between what and what Raper did not say, but probably between deviations from the trend lines, year by year.

It was a minor point, occupying barely a page, graph and all, stuck in between discussions of two entirely different subjects. Whether from caution or because he thought the mechanism was obvious, Raper did not even suggest how this cause-and-effect relationship might have come about.

A Statistical Celebrity

For a few years, the finding attracted little attention. It remained little more than an aside, in a book primarily of interest to those concerned with the grievous social problem it examined. In 1939, however, Hovland and Sears, psychologists at Yale's Institute of Human Relations, plucked the correlation from the obscurity of Raper's monograph, and its fame dates from their *Journal of Psychology* article.

Hovland and Sears placed the correlation in a theoretical context, like a diamond in a setting. The very title of their article, "Minor Studies of Aggression: VI," implied a larger research program. Moreover, the title was abstract, *conceptual:* only the subtitle mentioned anything as concrete as lynching or economic indices. Raper's correlation became not just an interesting fact about lynching but a statistical test of "the hypothesis that the strength of instigation to aggression varies directly with the amount of interference with the frustrated goal-response."

Hovland and Sears examined two dependent variables (total number of lynchings in the United States and lynchings of blacks) and three independent variables (per-acre value of cotton, total value of the cotton crop, and an index of total economic activity in the United States). (For their data on lynching Hovland and Sears did use Work's compilation, and, unlike Raper, cited it.) In each case but one—Ayre's Index of general economic activity was already expressed as deviations from a trend line—they computed deviations from a least-squares linear trend, fitted to the data for the entire forty-nine-year period, 1882–1930. Tetrachoric correlations between various combinations of these residuals gave negative values even larger than the one Raper had reported. The largest, that between the deviation from its trend line of the total value of the cotton crop and the deviation from *its* trend line of the number of blacks lynched, was –.72. (Notice, for future reference, how awkward it is to express this finding precisely.)

Reported in this context, by these authors, the correlation obviously struck a great many people's fancy. Even before the journal article appeared, it was cited in a volume surveying frustration-aggression theory and research, by John Dollard and other members of the Institute of Human Relations group to which Hovland and Sears belonged, and it soon made its way, for example, into Hadley Cantril's *Psychology of Social Movements* (1941) and S. H. Britt's *Social Psychology of Modern Life* (1941), the latter apparently the first of many textbooks it would adorn.

In a 1946 article in the *Journal of Abnormal and Social Psychology*, Alexander Mintz cites these three books as evidence of the correlation's acceptance but points out that all three misstate its findings. As we have seen, those findings are not easy to state. It is much easier to say that the article shows decreases in cotton prices to be associated with increases in the number of lynchings, or even just that it shows cotton prices and lynchings to be negatively correlated. Neither, in fact, is exactly what it does show, but each conveys the general idea.

Cold Water

But Mintz did not merely criticize the way the study's results had been summarized; he also took a close look at how they had been arrived at in the first place, and he did not like what he saw. He observed, in the first place, that there was no reason to assume that the underlying trends were linear; indeed, inspection of the data suggested that they were not. Moreover, the tetrachoric approximations to product-moment correlations that Hovland and Sears employed are accurate only under assumptions that did not appear to be met by their data. (Specifically, they assume homoscedasticity and normal distribution of the variables.) By choosing less arbitrary trend lines from which to compute deviations and by computing actual product-moment correlations rather than tetrachoric approximations, Mintz arrived at strikingly smaller associations. The correlation involving total number of lynchings and overall United States economic activity, $-.65$ by the Yale researchers' reckoning, was reduced to $-.28$ by Mintz's calculations. And the largest and most appealing correlation, that involving total value of the cotton crop and lynchings of blacks ($-.72$), essentially disappeared: Mintz's figure was a *positive* .014. By looking only at the period 1882–1913, Mintz could report a figure of –.25, but in the absence of any rationale for isolating those particular years, this sort of post hoc "adjustment" is unpersuasive.

All in all, Mintz's work leaves open the possibility of some modest linkage between economic conditions and lynching, but clearly the original, dramatic correlation had been a methodological artifact. In a 1954 survey article, Roger Brown concluded that Mintz's calculations had in fact "cast doubt on the reality of the relationship" altogether. Brown, however, is apparently one of the few who had noticed.

Life after Death

Despite Mintz's attempt to drive a stake through its heart, the cotton-and-lynching correlation would not die. Its recovery was well advanced by 1964 when Bernard Berelson and Gary A. Steiner published an encyclopedic inventory of "scientific findings" concerning human behavior. They reported the correlations from the original article, adding that "a later study reduced these correlations somewhat, but they still remained in effect." No wonder, perhaps, that when we surveyed our sample of SPSSI members, most did not know whether later research had supported Hovland and Sears, or that three-quarters of those who believed they did know, were wrong.

No wonder either that the correlation continues to wander, zombielike, through the social science literature. When we tracked down all references to Raper, Hovland and Sears, and Mintz in the *Social Science Citation Index* from 1969 to May 1985, we turned up a number of examples—some of them dismaying—from several disciplines.

Many simply write as if Mintz's article had never been published. Of nine citations we found to Hovland and Sears, only two mention Mintz's critique. Even those who cite Mintz usually miss his point. One researcher, for example, cites *only* Mintz, but in *support* of his assertion that "a close relationship [exists] between frustration and prejudice" (and also, oddly, that "individuals get more aggressive when the target person is disliked for his social visibility"). Perhaps even more bizarre, another reports the original correlation, notes that "the magnitude of the correlation has been disputed" (by Mintz), then asserts that "students of this issue . . . have concluded that at least some relation does exist between economic prosperity and lynching." The only "student of this issue" cited is Roger Brown, who in fact concluded nothing of the sort.

And nearly everyone who mentions Hovland and Sears at all continues to state incorrectly even what they thought they had shown. Most commonly, the problem is simply the one Mintz identified, that of failing to indicate that the correlations are between deviations from trend lines: for instance, "the celebrated study of Hovland and Sears . . . reported that the price of cotton in the southern United States (an index of economic prosperity) was negatively correlated with the lynchings of blacks." Sometimes, however, other errors creep in, as in: "the price of cotton is (or was) negatively correlated with the number of southern Negro lynchings." (Strictly speaking, Hovland and Sears examined *all* lynchings of Negroes, not just "southern" ones—although the great majority were in fact in the South.) And occasionally, the variations on the basic theme are downright baroque; for instance:

> Hovland and Sears . . . obtained indices (such as cotton prices) of economic conditions in the American South for the early half of the twentieth century. They then compared these indices with the number of lynchings of Negroes in the same area. Their findings indicated that the number of lynchings increased following economic downturns (the correlation between the cotton price index and lynchings was -0.72).

An exacting calculation would put the number of distinct misstatements of fact in those three sentences at five.

In general, the more vague the summary, the less likely it is to be in error, as when an article says merely that Hovland and Sears "linked economic frustrations to racial hostility." But even vagueness is no guarantee of accuracy. When one writer says that Hovland and Sears "suggested . . . that changes in the relative position of social and racial groups, or the threat thereof, leads to increased antagonism," she attributes to them a view that was not theirs: whites' *absolute* well-being, not their circumstances relative to blacks, is most obviously linked to changes in the price of cotton.

These misstatements are fairly minor, and their authors usually cite Hovland and Sears only in passing. It could certainly be argued that their errors are trivial and relatively benign. We do not assert that their conclusions are undermined by their accepting Hovland and Sears at face value, or even by accepting a distortion of their conclusion. We point to them only as illustrating and contributing to a situation where "everybody knows" something that is not exactly correct.

A Textbook Case

Perhaps more culpable are textbook writers who misuse this correlation. When we looked at fifty-odd recent texts in social psychology, general psychology, and sociology, we found ten that allude to the frustration-aggression interpretation of lynching. Except for one that contents itself with remarking that the theory "helps provide a uniform theoretical integration of aggressive phenomena as diverse as lynchings and violent fantasies," all use the Hovland and Sears "finding" as a major illustration of the theory. Since their use of the correlation is not at all incidental, they might be expected to subject it to skeptical scrutiny. But all state the correlation (or rather misstate it, to one degree or another) without qualifications or reservation; many cite the original, inflated correlations, and none urges caution. Only one of the ten books mentions Mintz's reexamination, and it says perversely that evidence for "a strong relationship between the price of cotton and the number of lynchings in the South during the years 1882 to 1930 [was] presented by Hovland and Sears (1940) and confirmed by Mintz (1946)."

We may suspect, without accusing anyone in particular, that textbook writers are borrowing examples from one another. As we have observed, this particular example is a striking and memorable one, especially when combined with attention-grabbing visuals (and at least two of these textbooks offer photographs of lynch-mob victims dangling from trees).

It is not our purpose to hold individuals up to scorn, or to cast stones at the gullible or careless. Rather, we offer these examples simply as additional da̤ta to support our contention that the *scientific* facts (as established by the original correlations reported by Hovland and Sears, and by Mintz's reassessment) have very little to do with what are now accepted as facts by the scientific community—in this case, by those lower orders of the scientific community to be found in undergraduate classrooms.

More Cold Water

One article we have not mentioned, published in 1969 in *Public Opinion Quarterly* by the senior author of this note (Reed), actually offers a capsule history of the correlation and remarks on its robust afterlife. It not only summarizes Mintz's empirical and methodological critique of the Hovland and Sears correlation, but it also challenges the dominant interpretation of what that correlation *means,* if indeed it exists.

The usual interpretation, as summarized by one of the textbooks, is that "when the price of cotton was low, white Southerners suffered economic hardship and frustration. Their aggression was displaced onto the black community." Or as another author put it, more colorfully: "Clearly [when cotton prices fell] the white sharecropper, faced with his decreasing ability to feed or clothe his family adequately, was resorting more and more to the donning of the white sheet, and taking out his rage and frustration on the helpless blacks."

But that explanation, this article points out, "is only one of several possibilities."

> The mechanism intervening between poor economic conditions and a high incidence of lynching could have been (1) white frustration, leading to displaced aggression—as [Hovland and Sears] argued; (2) Negro frustration, leading to aggressive acts, punishable by lynching—still relevant to their theoretical framework; or (3) Negro economic need, leading to crimes against property (with or without violence), punishable by lynching. That "lynchings do not arise out of an attempt to improve one's economic position during times of economic stress, as is the case with property crimes," as Hovland and

Sears note, does not mean that lynchings were not often the sequel to property crimes, as any reading of case histories will reveal.

Like Roger Brown's judicious summary of the evidence in the *Handbook of Social Psychology*, this article is one of a very few exceptions to the apparent rule that those who know of Mintz's article and understand it do not cite Hovland and Sears. In fact, it would not have cited Hovland and Sears at all—would not, that is, have been an exception—had not its author been asked to do so by the editor of the journal in which it appeared, on the grounds that omitting any reference to this well-known "fact" would strike readers as strange.

The resulting footnote may have struck some readers as strange—that is, as strangely irrelevant to the rest of the article, which dealt with another aspect of lynching altogether. It would be surprising if a mere footnote in an unrelated article had done anything to impede the spread of the folklore, and it apparently did not. Indeed, the only citation to this article for any reason, ever, anywhere, seems to be in a "comment" by Edward Tufte that questions its methodological soundness. This is, in fact, the only evidence that anyone aside from author and reviewers ever read it.

So What?

Our aim here, obviously, is not to challenge frustration-aggression theory. That theory plainly does not stand or fall on the existence of a single correlation. Nor do we wish to argue that lynching was not affected by economic conditions—even by cotton prices. In fact, we believe that it was, just not with the fine-tuned precision, and perhaps not entirely for the reason, that Hovland, Sears, and those who cite them have assumed. (For the record, *large* changes in cotton prices were often accompanied by appropriate changes in the number of lynchings—and for that conclusion it is difficult to improve on Raper's original graphic presentation of the data.)

We do believe, however, that the history of this correlation illustrates a problem in the operation of social science as a social institution. In science, in principle, a failure to replicate is as significant as the original finding, and perhaps more so. In practice, though, such

failures may not receive the same attention as a striking and successful test of a hypothesis. This may be especially so in cases like this
one, where the test makes a good story—"good" less in scientific
than in journalistic terms.

There is more to this than merely a restatement in a scientific
context of the journalistic truism that retractions rarely catch up with
original stories. Many articles and textbooks, of course, do not mention the cotton-and-lynching correlation at all, even where it would
be an appropriate illustration, if true. We cannot say with certainty
how many authors omit it because they believe it has been seriously
challenged, and how many because they never heard of it in the first
place (although our sample survey suggests that there are probably
far more of the latter). But since there is hardly any reason for anyone
to write that the correlation does *not* exist, the field is left almost
entirely to those who believe that it does.

In addition to this illustration of how science works as a collective
undertaking, there are some lessons here about how individual *scientists* work. This story may have a moral, if only the quotidian one
summed up in the famous advice attributed to Martin Routh, the
long-lived president of Magdalen College in the early 1800s. When an
admirer asked the ninety-two-year-old Routh for some axiom or
precept that he had found to be of special value in his long life of
scholarship, the old gentleman replied, "You will find it a very good
practice *always to verify your references,* sir!"

The Central Theme

Birthrate *Brown*-Out

with Ronald R. Rindfuss and Craig St. John

At a time in the 1950s when the overall birthrate in the United States was increasing sharply, the states of the South displayed a markedly lower increase, thereby closing, even reversing, a longstanding regional difference in fertility.[1] The most marked convergence between the South and the rest of the country occurred between 1954 and 1955 (see Figure 1). Ronald Rindfuss has written about the long-range change; the sharp shift in 1954 and 1955 is the subject of this report.

Because these fertility rates were computed from sample data from the 1960 and 1970 censuses, that shift was originally dismissed as due to random variation. Further inspection, however, revealed that the same pattern exists in the total number of births actually registered. We examined reported vital registration data for whites and blacks. In the South between 1953 and 1954, the number of white births increased faster than in the nation as a whole (2.2 percent in the South, .8 percent nationally), but between 1954 and 1955 it declined by .7 percent while the national figure was increasing by 1.9 percent. Between 1955 and 1956, the number of white births increased again in the South (by 2.2 percent) but more slowly than in the nation as a whole (the national increase was 2.6 percent). In 1955, twenty-three of the thirty-two non-Southern states had more white births than in 1954, whereas only four

1. The "South" here is the "census South," which includes the eleven former Confederate states plus Delaware, Maryland, West Virginia, Kentucky, Oklahoma, and the District of Columbia.

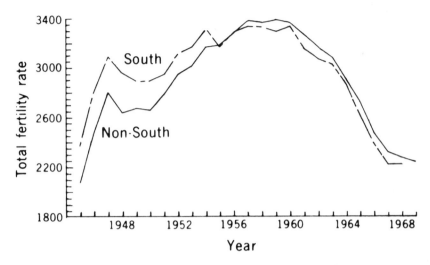

Figure 1. Total fertility rates of Southern and non-Southern women, 1945–1969. The total fertility rate is the number of children 1,000 women of childbearing age would be predicted to give birth to in their lifetimes if the fertility rate of the base period remained unchanged. (Figure courtesy of *Social Forces.*)

of the sixteen Southern states did. The year before, twenty-eight of the non-Southern states and fourteen of the Southern states had shown 'increases. The pattern of black births was similar but less pronounced.

Aberrant behavior in the South in the year 1954 is likely to suggest its own explanation to those familiar with the region's history. On May 17, 1954, the Supreme Court rendered its decision in *Brown v. Board of Education,* declaring public school segregation to be unconstitutional. It is clear that the court's unanimous decision struck at what many white Southerners saw as the basis of their region's way of life and that it came as a shock to many Southerners. (White Southern opposition to the decision hardly needs documenting, but in a sample survey two years after the Court's ruling only 14 percent of white residents of the census South expressed support for school desegregation.) It seems reasonable to entertain the conjecture that anomie and fear for the future led some Southerners to put off having children who would otherwise have been conceived during this period.[2]

2. Psychological stress can trigger physiological subfecundity by blocking the release of the luteinizing hormone necessary for ovulation. It can also reduce

First, the timing was right, roughly speaking. The effects of events in May and in the summer of 1954 would not show up in birth figures until 1955. Second, the slighter drop among blacks seems consistent with the hypothesis: although black Southerners also experienced uncertainty in the wake of the court's ruling (their traditional pattern of education was threatened, and undoubtedly they feared that violence might accompany desegregation), obviously the status and prerogatives of white Southerners were more clearly at stake.

Table 1 shows the pattern of change in numbers of births in relation to the existence of segregated schools. Of the eleven former Confederate states, all of which are included in almost any definition of the South, only two—North Carolina and Florida—had an increase in white births between 1954 and 1955. (Nine of the eleven had had an increase the year before, and nine had an increase the next year.) Six other states and the District of Columbia also required school segregation in 1954, but most of these had relatively small black populations and were less affected by the court's ruling. Three of these six states and the District of Columbia had fewer white births in 1955 than in 1954, and three had more. (In 1954 only the District of Columbia had fewer white births than in 1953. In 1956 only the District and Kentucky had fewer than in 1955.) Of the thirty-one other states, twenty-two had more white births in 1955 than in 1954; of the nine exceptions, three—Pennsylvania, Indiana, and Kansas (the state in which the *Brown* case originated)—had a noticeable degree of school segregation at the local level.[3] (In 1954, twenty-seven of the thirty-one had more white births than in 1953; in 1956, twenty-two had more white births than in 1955.)

---

male potency. But we are not suggesting that the *Brown* decision had those effects. We considered current events other than the court's decision as alternative explanations for the decline in Southern fertility. These ranged from Hurricane Hazel to the possibility of a short-run economic downturn in the South. Upon investigation, none of these alternative explanations seemed plausible.

3. Five of the other six were small states that exhibit considerable year-to-year fluctuation in number of births: Idaho, Maine, North Dakota, Rhode Island, and Wyoming.

Table 1. Direction of Change in Number of White Births between 1954 and 1955 in States with Dual School Systems and in the Other States.

State group	Number of *states with:*	
	Increase	Decrease
Former Confederate States	2	9
Other dual-system states and D.C.	3	4
Remaining states	22	9

We also compared 1954 and 1955 births grouped according to the age of the mother and to the birth order of the child. In every age group, the ratio of the number of births in 1955 to the number of births in 1954 was lower in the former Confederate states and in the other states with dual school systems than in the rest of the country. The same is true for birth order, with one exception: in all three groups of states there were declines in the number of second births from 1954 to 1955, and the decline was slightly smaller in the two groups of dual-system states than in the other states.

These differences between the states affected by the *Brown v. Board of Education* decision and those not affected by the decision do not in themselves, of course, establish a cause-and-effect relationship. Yet, it is a striking coincidence and one that gets more striking when we look at month-by-month data.

The earliest one could possibly expect to see any effect of the ruling on fertility would be in the early spring of 1955. Some couples who had not been practicing contraception might have begun to do so immediately after the Supreme Court decision. Some couples who had planned to stop using contraception in order to have babies might have decided not to stop. In either case, the effect on subsequent fertility levels would be gradual because of the time required to conceive in the absence of deliberate contraception. Also, it can be assumed that these hypothetical decisions would not have been made the day after the Supreme Court's decision, but that it would have taken a while for the implications of the decision to sink in. Finally, after it became clear that segregation would continue for some time, that life would go on much as usual, that "all deliberate speed" could be very deliberate, and that Southern politicians had some resources of their own to resist with—in other words, when it became clear that nothing much was going to change any time soon—our hypothetical couples would have resumed their normal fertility behavior, and the Southern white birthrate would have resumed its increase. Thus, the major depression in Southern white birthrates in reaction to the Supreme Court decision would be expected in the late spring or early summer of 1955, terminating shortly thereafter.

In Figure 2 we have plotted for the three groups of states discussed above the number of white births in each month of 1955, as a percentage of the number in the same month in 1954. This statistic, though crude, removes seasonal variation in birth rates (including variation due to differences in the number of days per month) and any differences among regions in that variation. In both sets of states with segregated schools we find a decrease in the number of white births beginning in late spring or early summer. In the summer both sets of states with segregated schools experienced lower fertility than the year before, but that was not the case in the rest of the United States. By the end of fall this relative depression in the number of births was essentially over in both groups of dual-system states. The reduction was somewhat greater and lasted somewhat longer in the former Confederate states than in the other dual-system states, as would be expected.

The pattern of month-by-month variation within individual states further supports the evidence of Figure 2. In order to reduce chance variation, we examined only the thirty-four states that averaged more than two thousand white births per month during this period. Of these, sixteen were dual-system states. All but two of the sixteen had fewer white births during the late spring and early summer of 1955 than in those periods in 1954. That was true of only seven of the eighteen unitary-system states, six of the seven being states that border on one or more of the dual-system states.

In other words, we find the number of white births in the South to

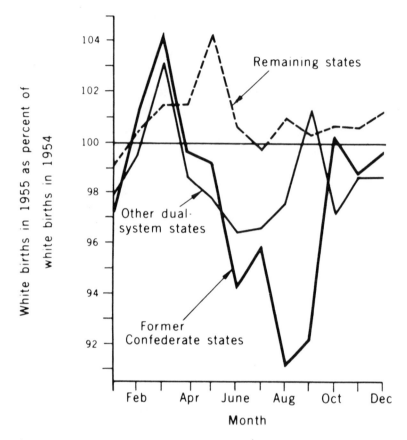

Figure 2.   White births in each month of 1955 as a percentage of white births in the same months of 1954, in states with dual school systems and in the other states.

be lower than expected at almost the exact time we would predict, assuming that the *Brown* decision demoralized prospective parents enough to cause some who would otherwise have stopped contraception to continue, and to cause others who had not been using contraception to begin.

The deflection is short-lived, concentrated in a period of three or four months. It is not large: Southern white birthrates were reduced by something on the order of 5 percent.[4] But even this small deflec-

4. But a deflection much greater would be literally incredible. The seasonally adjusted number of births in the former Confederate states for June 1955 was

tion is of considerable historical interest if one accepts our explanation of it. It may, in addition, have some implications beyond that—implications for the study of fertility trends elsewhere in the developed world and implications about the ability of social scientists to explain and predict such trends. Within the United States since World War II, for instance, there have been large, unprecedented, and unpredicted changes in fertility behavior, with significant consequences for many institutions in American society. The fact that these changes have been found within every social, economic, and racial group suggests that they cannot be accounted for by changes in the composition of the population and that their explanation must be linked to historical events.

---

slightly more than two standard deviations below the average number of births (seasonally adjusted) in those states for the previous thirteen months. (For August and September, the difference is even greater.) Alternatively, if chance variation were the only factor at work it would be unlikely that the two groups of dual-system states would show declines for April, May, June, and July of 1955 (relative to the same months of the previous year) while the rest of the country experienced increases.

Jim Crow, R.I.P.

with Merle Black

In 1942, only 2 percent of white Southerners responding to a survey by the National Opinion Research Center said that black and white children should attend the same schools.[1] The proportions in favor of desegregating public transportation and neighborhoods were almost as small: 4 percent and 12 percent, respectively. This was, for all intents and purposes, unanimity. White Southern opposition to desegregation was widely regarded as simply an immutable fact, one that would have to be reckoned with by anyone concerned to improve Southern race relations. It appeared to be true, as U. B. Phillips had written fourteen years earlier, that a determination that the South "be and remain a white man's country" was "the cardinal test of a Southerner." It went without saying, of course, that "a Southerner" was white.

It is true that white Southerners who supported segregation in 1942 were merely endorsing the existing state of affairs: in the case of schools and public transportation, arrangements required by law in most of the South. But in 1956, two years after *Brown v. Board of Education,* only 14 percent of Southern whites favored school desegregation. Reporting a study conducted as late as 1961, Donald Matthews and James Prothro concluded that "only a significant change in white racial attitudes, awareness, and expectations" could ensure

1. The study, reported by Hyman and Sheatsley, included as "Southerners" residents of Maryland, Delaware, West Virginia, and the District of Columbia.

"the prevention of a racial holocaust and the preservation of political democracy in the South." Nineteen years after *that,* however, in 1980, only one white Southern parent in twenty objected to sending a child to school with "a few" black children—supported school segregation, that is, *in principle.*[2] It is now impossible to find any body of respectable opinion willing to express support for de jure segregation.

This does not reflect a general increase in social liberalism. To take only one striking example, a study by Joseph E. Schneider of forty-one fundamentalist ministers in North Carolina, thirty-five of whom favored Senator Jesse Helms in the then-current senatorial election, classified three-quarters of them as "liberal" or "moderate" in their racial views. Most supported racial equality as a "Christian goal," and only a bare majority even opposed affirmative action (as a form of discrimination against whites). Several volunteered that they had come to admire Martin Luther King, Jr., after disliking him in the 1960s, and three independently volunteered that they occasionally rewrote King's sermons and preached them (presumably without their congregations' knowledge).

Even if there is an element of hypocrisy in these survey responses and these testimonials, even if people say what they think they ought to say and not what they really believe, it is significant that white Southerners now believe they ought not to object to desegregation. That itself is a change no one would have predicted in 1942.

Andrew Greeley has argued that this breaking up of an orthodoxy—not just the destruction of a consensus, but the emergence of a new, contradictory one—is "one of the most impressive social accomplishments of modern times." Certainly it is at least one of the most complete turnarounds in the history of public opinion polling. Moreover, in historical and comparative terms, it happened very quickly, and it can be argued that it came about at remarkably little cost.

2. These figures from the Gallup Organization are for white Southern parents, a less inclusive and a younger group than the NORC's general population sample. Gallup's "South" includes only the eleven former Confederate states plus Kentucky and Oklahoma. In the South, as elsewhere in the United States, white parents express greater opposition to sending children to schools where half or, especially, more than half of the students are black.

Table 1.   Southern White Parents Objecting to Desegregated Schools, 1958–1980. (Responses of non-Southern white parents presented for comparison.)

"Would you, yourself, have any objection to sending your children to a school where [a few] of the children are colored/Negroes/black?"

(percentage "yes")

Year	South	Non-South
1958	72	13
1959	72	7
1963	61	10
1965	37	7
1966	24	6
1969	21	7
1970	16	6
1973	16	6
1975	15	3
1978	7	4
1980	5	5

Source: *The Gallup Report,* no. 185 (February 1981): 30.

How did it happen? A closer examination of public opinion data allows us to locate the change more precisely in time. Table 1 shows the responses of white Southern parents to a question often repeated by the Gallup Poll between the late 1950s and 1980: "Would you, yourself, have any objection to sending your children to a school where a few of the children are black?"[3]

As the 1950s ended, white Southern support for school segregation was decreasing, although very slowly. In the late 1950s, three-quarters of white Southern parents still told the Gallup Poll that they did not

---

3. In earlier surveys: "colored" or "Negroes." These data are presented because they cover a longer period, in more detail, than other trend data available, but other data show much the same pattern.

want their children in school with even "a few" black classmates. (The difference between the 72 percent who did so in 1959 and the figure for non-Southern white parents—7 percent—must be one of the largest regional differences ever recorded by a public opinion poll.) By 1963, that figure had decreased somewhat, but three out of five Southern parents still objected.

In the three years from 1963 to 1966, however, the rate of change increased abruptly. Southern white parents' opposition to the presence of black children in their own children's schools decreased by 12 or 13 percent a year. In 1963, 61 percent were opposed, by 1965 only 37 percent, and by 1966 only 24 percent. Put another way: each year for three years, roughly a quarter of all remaining opponents dropped their opposition, and hard-core opposition to school desegregation became a minority view in the South as a whole. After 1966, the rate of change slowed, in part because there were so few supporters of outright segregation left who *could* change. But change merely slowed to something like its earlier rate; it did not stop altogether (and for the "white backlash" that received much media attention in the mid-1960s, there is no evidence whatsoever).

There are two separate phenomena here to be explained: first, the gradual, long-term erosion of support over the entire 40-year period; second, the abrupt collapse in the mid-1960s. Jim Crow's illness, that is, was chronic before it became acute, and terminal.

The long-term change in white Southern racial attitudes was slow (painfully slow, for those who desired it) but like a glacier: inexorably, year after year, it moved in the same direction. One reason for this, as Herbert H. Hyman and Paul B. Sheatsley observed in 1963, is that the trend was produced in part by massive economic and demographic changes taking place in the South. In 1942, support for segregation was virtually universal among white Southerners: no particular *kind* of white Southerner was much less likely to support it than any other kind. By the 1950s, however, support for segregation had become less common among educated Southerners, less common among urban Southerners, less common outside the conventionally defined *Deep* South, less common among those who had lived outside the South or were often exposed to the mass media—less common, in short, among the kinds of Southerners that urbanization and economic development were producing in ever-larger numbers.

Also contributing to the trend was what is known as "cohort succession"—a polite way of saying that some people were dying and being replaced by other people with different attitudes. Beginning in the 1950s, each new wave of young white adults adhered less staunchly to white Southern racial orthodoxy than the preceding generation (in part, but not entirely, because they were better-educated, more urban, and so forth). Most young people shared their parents' views, but when there was intergenerational disagreement it was nearly always in the same direction. Just as it was difficult in the 1950s and 1960s to find young Southerners with fewer years of schooling than their parents, so was it hard to find ones more committed to the defense of segregation. The cumulative effect over thirty or forty years was considerable. Even if no individual Southerner had ever changed his mind, white Southern public opinion as a whole would have changed.

Tidal processes like these cannot be expected to produce rapid change, and they did not. But the consequent erosion of support for de jure segregation anticipated the collapse of that support and may have made it possible. By the early 1960s, white Southern opinion was not unanimous, as it had been virtually twenty years before. A minority, substantial in some localities, favored desegregation or at least were resigned to the prospect. Even the opposition, although widespread, was no longer monolithically *determined.* Relatively few segregationists were willing (as their opponents in the civil rights movement were willing) to risk their lives, their freedom, their jobs, or even their comfort on behalf of their views. For many segregationist Southern whites, commitment to other values—to law and order, to the good repute of their communities, to economic development— interfered with their commitment to the preservation of racial segregation. Not many were willing to give up a great deal to preserve it.

For others, fatalism may have had the same result. A common cultural value among both black and white Southerners, fatalism has been most common among rural, poorly educated, older people: in those sectors of the population who, if white, were most likely to oppose desegregation.[4] Confronted with the prospect of change, many segregationists believed their cause was lost whatever they might do. They may not have been happy about what was going to happen, but they did not believe they could prevent it. Consequently, as one observer noted, during Little Rock's troubles 124,500 of the city's 125,000 citizens went about their business, then went home at night and watched the other five hundred on television. The political importance of ambivalence, resignation, and indifference should not be underestimated.

In fact, support for segregation was hollow at the core and ready to be kicked over. This is, of course, much clearer in retrospect than it was at the time. We should not forget the ever-present atmosphere of violence: the beatings, bombings, and murders, and the constant threat of more and worse. The Mississippi "Freedom Summer" of 1964 alone saw eighty beatings, thirty-five shootings, thirty-five church burnings, thirty house bombings, and six murders. Nor should we forget the courage it took to confront this sort of thing. Civil rights workers and organizers were men and women who were willing to give up a great deal for their beliefs.

But we should also recognize that violent resistance came only from a small minority of the opposition—one, moreover, that did not receive the unqualified and near-unanimous support from the white community that the equivalent (and almost certainly larger) minority did during Reconstruction. This relative absence of community support is reflected both in the different casualty rates and the different outcomes of these two periods of acute racial conflict in the South. Richard Maxwell Brown, a distinguished historian of American violence, emphasizes that the violence deployed against the civil rights movement, though brutal and terrifying (as it was meant to be), was seldom fatal. Brown estimates that the massive structure of Jim Crow law, designed to fix the shape of Southern race relations forever, was utterly destroyed at a cost of forty-four people killed during the entire course of the civil rights movement. Those killings must be added to

4. Matthews and Prothro found that segregationist whites expected more change, faster, than other whites.

Jim Crow's shameful due bill, but they must also be assessed by comparison to over thirty-seven hundred earlier deaths by lynching, not to mention the ghastly toll exacted by intercommunal violence elsewhere in the world.

Strategically, most white resistance to change in the South amounted to a holding action. White supremacy had not been an active, expansionist ideology for nearly a half century. For the most part, whites who opposed desegregation tried merely to hold their ground, not to roll back change that had already taken place. Their response was seldom counterattack, and it soon shifted from hard-fought defense to strategic withdrawal—retreat—to private schools, private clubs, and the like. This could be fairly characterized as a "no-win" strategy; it could even be argued that removing the most vociferous opponents of desegregation from the public arena where desegregation was taking place allowed the process to proceed more smoothly. (In some communities that withdrawal has now proven to be temporary, although in others, of course, it appears to be more or less permanent.)

The hollowness of much prosegregation sentiment was also indicated by how quickly a great many segregationists changed their minds. As the 1960s began, most white Southerners apparently did favor state-supported segregation; in much of the white South, that was the only acceptable position. Yet five or six years later, only a minority of white Southerners supported "strict segregation"—Jim Crow—and such support was well on the way to being the exclusive property of the white-supremacist lunatic fringe.

If attitudes are deeply rooted, embedded in a supporting ideology or serving important psychological functions, that sort of change does not take place readily. But Thomas Pettigrew argued as early as 1959 that most white Southerners' segregationist attitudes were not of this sort, that they reflected instead simple conformity to community norms. The rapidity of the subsequent change suggests that Pettigrew was right: for many, those views were conventional, unstudied, and subject to change in response to experience, new knowledge, and new circumstances.

Obviously, the early years of the civil rights movement in the South presented Southern whites with a great deal of new knowledge and experience to assimilate, and rapid attitude change soon followed. It seems unlikely that the movement's moral appeals persuaded a great many supporters of segregation to rethink their position. But one thing the movement undeniably did teach white Southerners was that Southern blacks were united in their opposition to Jim Crow.

It may be hard to believe at this remove, but many Southern whites had persuaded themselves and each other—they sincerely believed—that black Southerners did not object to segregation, and even that they preferred it. Sheatsley reports, for example, that in 1963 only 35 percent of white Southerners believed that "most Negroes feel strongly about [the] right to send children to the same schools as whites."[5] In the face of local demonstrations, often led by local ministers, it became more difficult (although demonstrably not impossible) to persist in that belief. Supporting segregation could no longer be seen as a matter of endorsing a polite biracial consensus; it became more clearly support for the naked imposition of inferior status on an unwilling people. Some did not shrink from that view of what they were about, but others did.

In addition, courteous, nonviolent, but courageous and firm insistence on the rights of American citizens demonstrably won for the civil rights movement the overwhelming support of non-Southern public opinion. With that support behind it, the federal government began increasingly to offer carrots and to brandish sticks, especially in the major legislation of the first two years of the Johnson administration. As the depth and consistency of the federal commitment grew, even those segregationists who were not initially fatalistic and resigned to change came to realize that they were simply outgunned (sometimes, as at Ole Miss, literally so). Quite late in the game, there was much disagreement among Southern whites about whether the changes taking place were a good thing or not, but by the mid-1960s there was little disagreement about their inevitability.[6] Part of the

5. Much larger proportions, around 80 percent, recognized by then that blacks "felt strongly" about voting rights and employment discrimination.

6. In 1971, for instance, the Survey of North Carolina showed that a substantial majority of white North Carolinians supported desegregation, but over 60 per-

change in public opinion in the 1960s no doubt reflects simply in-creasing, if grudging, acquiescence.

Finally, the actual changes brought about by the activities of the federal government and the civil rights movement undermined op-position. These changes "created facts." The destruction of an estab-lished and taken-for-granted social order is a disconcerting prospect at best; it can be a relief simply to have matters settled. Once deseg-regation had taken place, its *opponents* were the ones who wanted change, and whatever contribution temperamental conservatism had made to the defense of segregation it now made to the defense of a new status quo. That, at least, is one interpretation of the frequent finding in the survey data that those who had experienced deseg-regation were least likely to oppose it.

Moreover, the new status quo was one that white Southerners usually discovered that they could live with. Desegregation was sim-ply not as bad as many had feared it would be. It helped that deseg-regation usually proceeded by degrees. When desegregating public accommodations (usually the first step) turned out to be fairly pain-less, the prospect of school desegregation became somewhat less threatening.

It bears emphasizing that desegregation *could not* have been as bad as some feared. Howard W. Odum's *Race and Rumors of Race* is an instructive compilation of what many white Southerners believed about their black neighbors in the early 1940s. Many of those beliefs were still at large some years later, which helps to make sense of the fact (otherwise hard to credit) that the *Brown* decision apparently produced a measurable deflection in the white Southern birthrate. Many Southern whites were simply frightened by the prospect of an end to segregation—an end, after all, to the South as they knew it.

Without painting over the very real problems of human relations that remain in the South, it is certainly no exaggeration to say that the dismantling of de jure segregation has worked out far better than

---

cent felt that "the integration of schools is doing more harm than good." The swing group was made up of those who hoped desegregation would be best in the long run or believed it was the right thing to do, bad effects notwithstanding.

many—probably most—white Southerners feared it would. The situation is far from ideal, but it can be argued that black-white relations in the South are now different only in minor degree from those in any other part of the United States with a significant black population—and that they are as often better as worse.

As for school desegregation specifically, in both urban and rural areas with black majorities or near majorities (as in many cities elsewhere), the schools are essentially still, or once again, segregated. But to deny that segregation de facto is preferable to segregation de jure is, if nothing else, to reject the reasoning of the *Brown* decision. Moreover, in most parts of the South, in towns and rural areas where blacks are a significant presence but a minority, desegregation is an accomplished fact that no one seriously proposes to undo, and few would undo even if they could. On a day-to-day basis, race relations are among the least of the problems most of these school systems face.

Speculation about the reasons for this success (and we should not hesitate to call it that) would have to include such factors as the community pride, athletic fanaticism, and traditions of civility common to many Southerners, both black and white. In addition, many have suggested that the cultural gulf between blacks and whites may be smaller in the South than elsewhere in the United States. Similar accents, similar tastes in recreation, similar forms of Evangelical Protestantism—these commonalities and others certainly do no harm, and their absence can. Ironically, it may even be that the South's tradition of color-conscious policy has helped it to deal with post–civil rights era realities. White Southerners, after all, have never even *pretended* to be color-blind, and where desegregation has worked well it has been attended by sensitivity to group interests, even by racial quotas (in such symbolically vital matters as selecting cheerleaders).

It is often said that morality cannot be legislated, and the example of Prohibition is usually adduced to prove it. But here is a case in which, to put it bluntly, a fundamental change in behavior was successfully imposed on a largely recalcitrant population. The happy outcome has been that most have decided the change was for the best.

Paul Sheatsley wrote in the mid-1960s that most white Americans know "that racial discrimination is morally wrong and recognize the legitimacy of the Negro protest." "In their hearts," he concluded, "they know that the American Negro is right." Sheatsley was writing about white Americans in general: it is unlikely that many white Southerners in fact knew anything of the sort at the time. But they know it now. Whatever else the civil rights movement may have accomplished or failed to accomplish, that achievement will stand.

Up from Segregation

Around 1970, a number of Southerners began to say something rather odd. Independently they had concluded that the South might be coming out of a tense and turbulent era in black-white relations in better condition than the rest of the country. Some even ventured to hope that the South could show other Americans, and the world, what an equitable biracial society looks like. The then-governor of Virginia, Linwood Holton, for instance, told a Rotary convention in St. Augustine, "We in the South have a better opportunity than any area of America to resolve the American dilemma, to become a model for race relations." Other observers—journalists and scholars as well as politicians—were starting to express similar opinions. It was about that time that I wrote an article with the self-explanatory title, "Can the South Show the Way?"

As the 1970s began, black Southerners were worse off than non-Southern blacks by nearly every measure one might examine: the standard of living they were able to achieve, their influence in politics, the white attitudes they confronted. But, I argued, their circumstances were improving faster in all of these respects. This had two important implications. In the first place, it helped to explain the otherwise puzzling fact that one opinion poll after another, throughout the 1960s, had shown that "Southern blacks [were] less resentful, more hopeful, and less alienated than other black Americans." People evaluate their situation not only in terms of how good or bad it is, but in light of how it is changing, and how rapidly. Things were clearly getting better for Southern blacks, and the polls showed that they recognized this. Consequently, they showed a degree of satisfaction to which many non-Southern blacks (for whom things were not improving as fast, if at all) were not disposed. This translated into a degree of patience, I wrote, that gave Southern whites the chance to make change "gracefully, in an atmosphere relatively free of urgency and acrimony."

The other implication, by simple arithmetic, was that the condition of black Southerners would soon be better than that of non-Southern blacks *in absolute terms*. I hedged: "The question is what the limits of these changes are to be. Straightforward extrapolation suggests that Southern blacks will soon be better off . . . than Northern black people; cynicism suggests that this is too much to hope for, and that [white Southerners] should be content with a pattern of race relations and racial inequalities no worse than that found elsewhere."

I do not know what Governor Holton's audience made of his speech, but the response to my article was . . . mixed. Some conservatives liked its insistence that the North was far from perfection in racial matters because it supported their view that Northerners ought to leave the South alone and put their own house in order. But others did not care for the assumption that white supremacy was doomed; they were not hog-wild about biracial societies in the first place and equitable ones least of all. A few liberals seemed to like the article because it could be used to shame Northerners ("If even the South can have good race relations, surely we can do better"), but others disliked what they saw as my complacence; they pointed out that the trends I was so cold-bloodedly examining did not just happen but were the product of struggle and sacrifice. Other liberals apparently felt the South did not *deserve* good race relations, and still others were damned if they were going to agree with any article published in *National Review,* as mine was.

All in all, however, the world little noted nor long remembered that article. I am still fond of it, though, not just because it was my first effort at political journalism but because its predictions increasingly look to be right.

Even at the time, although nobody knew it, black Americans were beginning to vote with their feet. In the early 1970s, for the first time since the end of the slave trade, more blacks moved to the South than left it—a pattern that continues. As an expanding economy and the death of Jim Crow have created a black middle class in the South alongside the old segregated triad of preacher, teacher, and undertaker, black managers and professionals have been moving to the South's cities and suburbs. The ingathering has been taking place at the bottom of the economic ladder, too, although there it is often not a matter of Southern promise but of crushed hopes in the North: poverty in rural Mississippi is at least safer and warmer than poverty in a Northern ghetto.

The pattern I noted of greater satisfaction and less impatience among Southern blacks has continued. A University of Michigan survey in 1978, for instance, found blacks in the South more likely than those elsewhere to say they were "completely satisfied with life": one non-Southern black in five said that, but one out of every three black Southerners said so. In part, this simply indicates that Southern blacks are good Southerners, since the same regional difference exists among whites. But the difference was greater among blacks than among whites; Southern blacks were more likely to express satisfaction than whites from any region; and the difference between Southern and non-Southern blacks was greater in 1978 than it had been seven years earlier. Those data suggest that black Southerners were still more likely to believe their conditions were improving.

If that is what they thought, they were correct. We can look in more detail at three ways that their situation was changing, corresponding roughly to what Max Weber identified as the three ways someone's situation *can* improve or deteriorate: one can have more or less money, power, and respect.

Money is the easiest to deal with since it lends itself best to counting. In 1970 Southern blacks were (as they always had been) poorer, on the average, than blacks in any other part of the country. Black Southern families were nearly twice as likely to be poor as black families in every other region of the United States. The gap was shrinking, but one could not expect it to close immediately. Part of the problem had to do with the South's economy: white incomes were lower in the South, too. And black Southerners of the older generation carried the burden of past discrimination: they had, on average, poorer education and less of it than blacks elsewhere in the country, and they were already in worse-paying jobs, with little likelihood that would soon change.

Despite all of the built-in inertia, though, the gap continued to close, and in 1982, for the first time, the poverty rate for black families in the South was no longer the highest in the country. It was still higher than that for black families in the Northeast or the West, but it was lower than in the North Central states—and that is something truly unprecedented. Figures for family income show the same convergence. In 1982, black family income in the South averaged about $13,000—some 5 percent higher than the figure for the North Central states.

Obviously, many Southern blacks still have economic problems, but their problems are now no worse than those of black families everywhere else in the nation. In part, unfortunately, this is because the situation of blacks elsewhere has deteriorated. During the twelve years from 1970 to 1982, the percentage of black families living in poverty decreased by five points in the South, while it was increasing everywhere else: by fourteen points in the North Central states, by twelve points in the Northeast, and by two and a half points in the West. In the mid-1980s, 38 percent of black families in the South were poor—a disgraceful figure, but that percentage was decreasing and was already lower than the figure for one other major American region. Black poverty is a serious problem, but my point here is that it is no longer a peculiarly *Southern* problem.

Moreover, the South may be better equipped than some other parts of the country to deal with it. If so, the trend should continue. The Sun Belt is not wholly a fiction, and the economic prospects for the South are certainly rosier than those for the cities of the Northeast and North Central states, where most blacks outside the South live. It has often been observed that a no-growth economy means one group can improve its condition only at the expense of another, which quite naturally resents and resists that improvement; in an expanding economy, though, one group can improve faster than another without anyone particularly noticing. If the South's economy continues to generate new jobs, some at least will go to black Southerners, and some benefits will trickle down (probably an accurate phrase) to those who are now the poorest—the economically marginal rural black population of the Deep South. Finally, it is ironic that the weakness of labor unions in the South, which some see as an unmistakable mark of Southern backwardness, may work to at least the short-run advantage of Southern blacks. Elsewhere, unions may have kept up the wages of those who had jobs, but it seems likely that they have reduced the total number of jobs available, and they have often operated, one way or another, to exclude blacks from employment.

When we turn from economics to politics, we see the same pattern, but even more dramatic: faster improvement, and in some respects a better situation, for blacks in the South. Here one finds an especially striking discontinuity, and it can be dated precisely: 1965. The Voting Rights Act of that year is arguably the single most important accomplishment of the entire civil rights movement.

In 1960, a mere quarter of the eligible black voters in the eleven formerly Confederate states were registered to vote. The poll taxes, literacy tests, and other devices that kept that figure low are a matter of public record; the economic and sometimes physical intimidation used for the same purpose usually operated less conspicuously. In 1964, well into the era of the civil rights movement, that figure had increased from 25 percent or so to only 38 percent, and in some states, of course, it was much lower. In Mississippi only 6 percent of eligible blacks were registered in 1965. By 1968, three years after the passage of the Voting Rights Act, the black registration percentage had increased from 38 percent to 62 percent in the South as a whole, and from 6 percent to nearly 60 percent in Mississippi. That percentage has not changed greatly since—it went up a little more by 1970 and subsequently decreased a bit—but it is almost as high as the percentage of whites registered to vote; it is about the same as the figure for black registration in the rest of the country; and it is high enough to have transformed Southern politics.

The most conspicuous change has probably been the election of blacks to public office in the South. There are tens of thousands of elected officials in the South, serving in the United States Congress and state legislatures, in city and county offices, in law enforcement, and on state and local school boards. In 1965, of these tens of thousands precisely 78 were black. By 1970, when Governor Holton made his speech and I wrote that article, there had been a ninefold increase to 711. By 1981, that figure had more than trebled: more than 2,500 blacks held elective office in the eleven ex-Confederate states, and Mississippi had more black elected officials than any other state in the Union. The number has continued to climb since then.

Between 1970 and the 1984 presidential campaign of Jesse Jackson, there was no increase in the percentage of Southern blacks registered to vote, so the growing number of black politicians in the South clearly indicates the growing political sophistication of the region's black voters. (Still, registration does no good without voter turnout. Here, too, though, there are encouraging portents for those who believe that black political participation indicates a healthy body politic. In the Democratic primaries on "Super Tuesday," March 13, 1984, black Southern Democrats were half again as likely as white ones to vote. Their votes delivered Georgia and Alabama to Walter Mondale and kept Jesse Jackson's candidacy alive.)

While the number and percentage of black elected officials in the South continues to grow, there is still a disparity between the percentage of black population and the percentage of black elected officials. Although blacks are about 19 percent of the South's population, only 3 percent or so of the South's elected officials are black. But in the Northeast only one-half of 1 percent of elected officials are black; in the North Central states and in the West, four-tenths of 1 percent. Put another way: twenty-two of every hundred thousand black Southerners are elected public officials. In the North Central states, the figure is nineteen per hundred thousand, in the West, fifteen, and in the Northeast, twelve.

Here again, there is little cause for Southern self-congratulation. Whites are much more likely than blacks to hold public office in the South, and the number and variety of ingenious schemes to keep it that way may well merit the attention of the Justice Department. But blacks are now less underrepresented than in other parts of the country; that is a remarkable change, and that is my point.

This is not because Southern whites are more willing than non-Southern whites to vote for black politicians. Public opinion polls and election results reveal no such difference. In the South, like everywhere else in the country, most elected black politicians represent constituencies with black majorities or close to it. But there are many more such constituencies in the South. The same concentration of black voting strength has drastically affected the behavior of white elected officials, even when it has not produced black officeholders. Southern white politicians are much more likely now to respond to the interests of their black constituents. Black enfranchisement has produced new faces: Jimmy Carter may be the epitome, but there are many others. In other cases, the new faces have been affixed to old heads. Think only of George Wallace's last gubernatorial race or Strom Thurmond's sponsorship of National Historically Black Colleges Week. (It is probably unkind to point out that the senator has always been in favor of black colleges.)

Political predictions are even riskier than economic ones, but there are some reasons to expect these trends to continue. In the Every-Cloud-Has-a-Silver-Lining Department, the increasing segregation of the South's cities means that more and more of them, like more and more cities elsewhere, will find themselves with black mayors and city councils (although a variety of redistricting and municipal reorganization schemes—all under intense judicial scrutiny—could affect this one way or the other). Less troublesome is what may be the increasing willingness of some white voters to support some black candidates. Charlotte is only one in a long string of Southern communities where black officeholders have been elected by biracial majorities. For the time being, at least, these majorities seem to result from the so-called "Atlanta coalition" between blacks and middle-class whites, rather than the populist coalition of have-nots that Chandler Davidson claims in his book, *Biracial Politics,* to have spied once in Houston.

When we turn from considerations of money and power to matters of respect, the problem of measuring well-being gets even trickier, but what we are talking about here is essentially the attitudes of white Southerners toward their black fellow citizens, and we can turn to opinion polls, with all their problems, for at least a first approximation. Here again, we find the familiar pattern of faster change in the South than elsewhere, leading to regional convergence.

Consider where we started. In 1942, public opinion polls showed that 98 percent of white Southerners favored absolute segregation of the public schools. *Ninety-eight percent.* That's everybody. (Two percent probably misunderstood the question.) By 1956, two years after the *Brown* decision, there had been only a little change in white Southern opinion: 14 percent of whites from the Southern and border states thought black and white children should attend the same schools. But by 1970, only 16 percent of white Southern parents—one in six—objected to having their children in school with "a few" black children, and this trend, too, has continued. By 1980, only 5 percent of white Southern parents said they did not want their children in school with any black children. Again, that is practically unanimous, but on the other side, and that number—5 percent—is no different from the figure for the country as a whole.

Imagine: a regional difference of great—indeed, calamitous—importance thirty years ago has simply evaporated, or so it appears. Of course, some of these people are lying: it was not entirely respectable in the 1980s to express segregationist views to a stranger who turns up on your doorstep. But in 1942, and 1956, it was not respectable *not* to express such views. And that, too, is a change of great importance.

There are still some regional differences in other measures of racial attitudes. White Southern parents are more likely than white parents elsewhere to say they do not want their children in schools with a black majority, for instance. But the regional difference is small, and most white parents everywhere say they would object to that. White Southerners are somewhat less likely than other whites to say they would vote for a qualified black presidential candidate, but most say they would. Most white Southerners say they do not approve of racial intermarriage, but almost as large a majority of non-Southern whites say that. All in all, the differences in racial attitudes between white Southerners and other white Americans are now differences only of degree, and of relatively small degree at that. Those differences are smaller than they have been at any time in the recent past, and they are getting smaller still each year.

In practice, I doubt that these remaining differences mean much. In the first place, what matters to non-Southern black people, day to day, is less the attitudes of all non-Southern whites than those of whites in the large cities of the Northeast and Midwest, where most blacks outside the South actually live. What whites in Vermont or Oregon think about race relations is of some academic interest, and occasionally of political importance, but it has little to do with the everyday experience of black Americans. I have not seen the attitudes of whites in Chicago, say, or Boston, broken out separately in attitude surveys, but surely few would care to argue that they are good examples for white Southerners to emulate.

In the second place, and more important, the attitudes someone expresses to a survey researcher are only part of the story and often not the most important part. The norms, the customs, that govern interaction can be as important as your attitudes in determining how you treat somebody. We saw how this worked under Jim Crow: how a white person felt about black people (or vice versa) had very little to do with how they interacted. That was prescribed in detail by an "etiquette of race relations" (to borrow the title of Bertram Doyle's 1937 book on the subject); individuals could only embroider the basic pattern a bit to suit their attitudes.

Perhaps I should say that *some* of us saw how it worked under Jim Crow. It bears emphasizing that the great majority of Southerners, black and white, are too young to remember *Brown v. Board of Education.* Those Southerners who did not live through the civil rights movement—my students, for example, who have a way of being born a bit later each year—find it hard to believe what most of us took for granted as just the way things were in the 1940s and 1950s. My students find it hilarious when I tell them that the *Brown* decision apparently produced a measurable deflection in the white Southern birthrate, or when they read in Howard Odum's *Race and Rumors of Race* about the "Eleanor [Roosevelt] Clubs" that many Southern whites believed their black maids belonged to. The splendid anthropological studies of the Jim Crow South have about as much immediacy for them, I would guess, as Malinowski on the Trobrianders. When I describe the segregated bathrooms and water fountains and dry cleaners and basketball teams of my youth, they appear to believe me—just as one would believe a Martian's description of his home planet. I gather that their parents, as a rule, do not talk about it.

It gives me some sympathy for immigrant parents who have to deal with American children. Southerners born before 1950 or so have "immigrated," in effect, just by staying put. The South we grew up in is as different from our children's as the Polish shtetl from Manhattan's Lower East Side or Naples from Boston's North End.

Even those who remember sometimes find it hard to believe. At least I do. A few years ago I saw a couple of etched glass doors in a small South Carolina town: one said WHITE, the other COLORED. I was almost literally stunned—stunned to realize that signs like that had once been an ordinary part of my life, and stunned to realize that it had been twenty years since I had last seen any. Like so much that was once thought to be terribly important, they had disappeared largely without my noticing. It is a nice touch, I think, that these doors that year were in an antique shop. If the dealer had not wanted fifty dollars for the pair I would have bought them. God only knows what for—maybe I would have used them in my teaching and taken an income-tax deduction.

Obviously things have changed. Laws have changed, and attitudes have changed, and (to return to the point) *etiquette* has changed. A while back, I had to do business in the courthouse of one of the poorest and blackest of North Carolina's counties. Ahead of me in line for the tax clerk was an elderly black man. In 1960, he would have automatically effaced himself, and I would just as automatically have gone ahead of him. I cannot say what he would have been thinking, but I probably would not have noticed. When his turn came, the young white woman at the counter would have addressed him as "James." She would not have meant to demean him, and, like me, she would not have been thinking about the implications of her behavior. Indeed, she would probably have denied that her behavior *had* any implications. She and I—and he, for that matter—would just have been doing what we were supposed to do, and our attitudes would have been neither here nor there.

That is not, obviously, what happened in 1984. I dare say that if Gallup ever came to that county, he would not find it a hotbed of racial liberalism. If he interviewed the young woman at the counter, I doubt that her attitudes would satisfy the sponsors of National Brotherhood Week. But in 1984 she waited on the man in his turn, exchanged some routine pleasantries with him about the unpleasant weather, called him "sir" at first and "Mr. Jones" after that—she treated him, in other words, like any other presumptively decent citizen of that county—and she was just doing what she was supposed to do.

Argument from anecdote is bad form in my trade, and I will not let my students do it, but I do believe that episode is increasingly typical. Manners *have* changed. More and more, in places like courthouses and stores and schools, Southern whites seem disposed to treat black Southerners as sort of honorary white folks—and by and large, whatever their private opinions of one another, white Southerners treat each other with courtesy and at least the appearance of good-natured respect. Southern blacks, for their part, seem willing to return the favor. The upshot is that on a day-to-day basis (which is how most of us lead our lives, after all) black-white relations in the South seem more cordial, less prickly, than black-white relations in the cities of the North. There is even some survey evidence to support this (again, from the University of Michigan): overall, 44 percent of non-Southerners described their lives as "very friendly"; 54 percent of all Southerners—and 58 percent of black Southerners—did so.

There is an irony here. William Chafe, in his study of the civil rights movement in Greensboro, *Civilities and Civil Rights,* argues that the value Southerners place on civility worked against the movement—to oversimplify his point, that even blacks' potential allies in the white community saw sit-ins and other forms of black protest and self-assertion as a violation of the norms of civility, as *bad manners*. If I am right, those same norms may contribute to amicable race relations today and in the future. Walker Percy has written somewhere that Southerners know the point of manners: they exist so that no one will not know what to do. A great many Southerners are apparently willing to do whatever they are supposed to do, and that can contribute to good race relations as easily as to bad.

No doubt some would argue that the value of civility still keeps many unresolved issues from being addressed squarely, and they may be right. One should recognize, though, that it is not just *white* Southerners who value civility. That black Southerners for a time were not willing to do what they were "supposed to do" does not indicate that they do not share that value; instead, their actions were dramatic evidence of the extent of their frustration and exasperation.

One more story. At a time when Chicago was disgracing itself with a bitter black-against-white mayoralty campaign, Harvey Gantt, who was running for mayor of Charlotte, said that race would not be the same sort of issue there. "We're much politer here," he told the *North Carolina Independent.* "We're not going to see that kind of down-in-the-gutter fight." He was right: Charlotte did not, and he soon became Charlotte's first black mayor.

Gantt's choice of pronouns points to another change that anyone who wishes the South well must welcome. Notice who is more polite: it is *we* (Southerners), not *they* (whites). This supports the observation by William Ferris, director of the Center for the Study of Southern Culture, that "what we're seeing is an interesting kind of evolution . . . to a sense of Southerners as Southerners as opposed to black versus white."

Now, some days I am more ready to believe that than others, but certainly there have always been similarities of style and culture between black and white Southerners. How could it be otherwise? (One frivolous example: On television recently I saw the Mighty Reverend Al Greene lead the Soul Train Dancers in a remarkable rendition of "Amazing Grace." The very next day, on the radio, I heard Jerry Lee Lewis swing directly from "Great Balls of Fire" to "If We Could Spend Our Vacation in Heaven." Which better illustrates W. J. Cash's observation about the mixture of hedonism and piety in the Southern mind?) Despite this cultural similarity, however, Southern blacks have not generally been inclined or encouraged in the past to think of themselves as black *Southerners,* and there is survey evidence to show that as late as the 1960s most probably did not.

Still, there have been dramatic changes since then, as Merle Black and I showed a while back in the *Journal of Politics.* If one wants to look for them, there are indeed signs of a sense of regional identification that increasingly transcends racial differences. That really is something new—and something wholly delightful, in my view.

To repeat the question some of us were asking circa 1970: Can the South show the way? Can the South, I wondered then, "do more than catch up with the Northern pattern of race relations?" Can it "break through to an accommodation qualitatively different from and superior to that displayed in, say, Philadelphia or Cicero?"

Well, perhaps it is beginning to. It is not really for me or for any other white Southerner to say whether the South has already become a better place than the Northeast or Midwest for black Americans to live, but it is certainly a better place now than it was in 1950, or 1970, and that may not be true of some other parts of the United States. The South has not shown the way yet. Black Southerners still have many legitimate grievances. They still do not have their share of money, power, and respect. But at least there is no reason for Southerners to apologize to Yankees anymore.

There is, to repeat, no reason to be smug about it. Catching up with the rest of the country is not an especially impressive achievement, and only a few white Southerners can take much credit even for that. But black Southerners can be proud of their accomplishment, and they have served their region—our region—well. The South is now more worthy than ever of Southerners' affection for it.

Those of us who predicted that in the early 1970s have no reason to be smug either. Leslie W. Dunbar predicted the same thing a decade earlier, in 1961, at a time when it sounded not just unlikely but downright crazy. Dunbar, executive director of the Southern Regional Council (the South's oldest biracial organization), had no illusions about his fellow white Southerners. He knew that white supremacy would not be given up without a fight, less because Southern whites profited from it than because many would feel it a duty to defend their past and their society. But Dunbar wrote:

> Once the fight is decisively lost (the verdict has to be decisive), once the Negro has secured the right to vote, has gained admittance to the public library, has fought into a desegregated public school, has been permitted to sup at a lunch counter, the typical white Southerner will shrug his shoulders, resume his stride, and go on. He has, after all, shared a land with his black neighbors for a long while; he can manage well enough even if the patterns change. There is now one fewer fight which history requires of him. He has done his ancestral duty. He . . . can relax a bit more.

And so, surprisingly enough, it has come to pass. The South has taken on a new character, as Dunbar said it would. Despite the conflict and turmoil since he wrote—indeed, largely because of it— the South still has the opportunity he saw a generation ago, one "it can fulfill better than any place or people anywhere." The South may yet "give the world its first grand example of two races of men living together in equality and with mutual respect."

Reflections

On Narrative and Sociology

Hermann Göring is supposed to have said, "When I hear the word 'culture' I reach for my revolver," and some feel that way these days about the word *narrative*. But they can hold their fire: I will be talking here about narrative in the simple, old-fashioned sense of storytelling, not about the Paris fashions modish these days in New Haven and Berkeley and the intellectual suburbs—not semiotics, hermeneutics, or any of the other tics of humanistic inquiry in these latter days. True, by undermining the authority of established forms of discourse, including scientific discourse, literary theorists may have given my theme an odd new respectability. But let them remain shadowy presences on the edge of this discussion. You can treat my homily as either old-fashioned or au courant, as you choose.

I have two major contentions. The first is that we sociologists do not give enough attention to narrative skill in graduate training, in manuscript evaluation, or in hiring and promotion decisions. My second, maybe more controversial, is that we should place more value on descriptive, interpretive, storytelling sociological work, for reasons both intellectual and (broadly speaking) political—and I cannot resist suggesting that there may be something "Southern" about this way of doing sociology. It may already be obvious that this address is going to be self-exemplifying: discursive, reflective, allusive—not hypothetico-deductive or even particularly focused. I even have a few stories to tell.

Poor Writing in Sociology

That the standard of writing in our discipline is appallingly low surely needs no documentation. Will you take the word for it of the book review editor of *Social Forces,* someone who has been reading raw sociological prose almost daily for seventeen years? Many have complained about this in the past, and it does not need just to be demonstrated once again; instead, I want to ask why it is the way it is and to say why we should concern ourselves with doing something about it.

Sociologists are not uniquely lame writers, to be sure. We can take a certain grim pleasure from recent developments in literary criticism, for instance, which demonstrate that professors of English can write worse prose than we ever dreamed of. And listen to Walter Laqueur, bemoaning the current state of historical writing: "The pendulum in the profession has been swinging . . . against descriptive, well-written books. There is nowadays a heavy preoccupation with methodology, with many footnotes and other academic trappings, and the writing often is lifeless and colorless."

Laqueur was writing in 1988, but historians have been complaining about this for a long time. Going on fifty years ago, for instance, Samuel Eliot Morison quoted Isaiah 22:5, "For it is a day of trouble, and of treading down, and of perplexity," and grumbled that modern historians would feel they were shortchanging their readers unless they wrote: "It is an era of agitation, of a progressive decline in the standard of living, and of uncertainty as to the correct policy."

Lamentations about scholarly writing are probably almost as old as scholarly writing itself, and old-timers always and everywhere believe that standards are declining. But the keepers of the standards often single out sociology and the other social sciences for special attention—and with reason. You may recall the game C. Wright Mills played with Talcott Parsons in *The Sociological Imagination,* where he took two pages of swampy Parsonsian prose and summarized it neatly in a paragraph, claiming to have made Parsons's point more clearly with no discernable loss of sense. And how many know the similar hatchet-job that H. L. Mencken did on Thorstein Veblen, pruning two of Veblen's paragraphs to a single sentence?

This tradition of sociology-bashing is still lively. In a 1987 *Virginia Quarterly Review,* Burling Lowrey quoted this sentence from a sociological monograph: "People drink alcohol in company because by depressing the inhibitory centers of the brain, it facilitates the friendly reciprocal stimulation on a relatively high level of emotionality which is the essence of leisure sociability." Lowrey claims that this means simply: "Drunks have more fun."

Well, not much is lost in translation, but if you look closely maybe you can find something. And certainly, as Kai Erikson has pointed out (and with more authority because he writes well himself), much criticism of this sort is unfair, inaccurate, or uninformed. We are entitled to technical terms, to precision, to complication when what we are talking about is complicated. Still, it is perfectly obvious that sociological prose is often more difficult than it has to be. Why is that?

One theory unkindly suggests that sociologists do not want to be understood. Recall that the word *gibberish,* by one account, comes from the eighth-century alchemist Jabir ibn Hayyan, who wrote obscurely for fear of being executed as a magician. Are we afraid of something? Listen to Mencken's assessment of Veblen:

> His ideas, in the main, were quite simple, and often anything but revolutionary in essence. What was genuinely remarkable about them was not their novelty, or their complexity, nor even the fact that a professor should harbor them; it was the astoundingly grandiose and rococo manner of their statement, the almost unbelievable tediousness and flatulence of the gifted headmaster's prose, his unprecedented talent for saying nothing in an august and heroic manner.

And Mencken was just getting warmed up. He went on, with his characteristic restraint, to characterize Veblen's "incredibly obscure and malodorous style" as "a relentless disease, a sort of progressive intellectual diabetes."

Sir Ernest Gowers (whose book *Plain Words* ought to be at every writer's elbow) echoes Mencken's implicit hypothesis, suggesting that "obscure and pretentious writing," using "convoluted sentences filled with technical terms," comes from those who "are afraid that if they write simply their readers will think the subject matter is simple, too." Appealing as this explanation may be, though, we know that most sociologists do not intend to mystify outsiders, not to mention each other.

No, sometimes unintelligibility comes from not knowing how to communicate clearly; sometimes from indifference, from not taking pains; sometimes from a desire to tell other insiders by style and choice of words that one is an insider, too. Not knowing how to write clearly is a matter of training; not caring to do so is a matter of reward structures. In other words, we are not taught to do it, and even if we know how, there is little pay-off for it. (There may even be some rewards for a particular kind of bad writing. I will come back to that.)

About our lack of attention to training in writing there is little to be said. We do not teach graduate students to write well; in fact, we seem to teach them somehow—by example, I fear—to write poorly. It is a common observation that our graduate students write less well after four or five or six years of graduate school than they did when they entered.

This problem, to repeat, comes from neglect, not intent. In her book *Practicing History,* Barbara Tuchman pointed to three aspects of being a historian: the investigative, the didactic, and the narrative, each of which involves skills that must be taught. The sociological equivalents might be, approximately, training in research methods, in theory, and in communication— and just putting it that way emphasizes our neglect of the last.

To be sure, communication is useless without something to communicate, which is why I think the motto of the Southern Sociological Society, "Docemus, quaerimus" ("We teach, we inquire") puts the cart before the horse by putting teaching before inquiry. Of course, it could be freely translated as "We teach, we ask questions" (that is, on examinations), an all-too-accurate description of how many of us spend our time.

Anyway, communication certainly is a means, not an end. But since science is a social undertaking, it is equally certain that research and theoretical activity are useless unless somehow communicated through writing or lecturing. Indeed, there is a sense in which sociology does not exist until it is shared. And we are sadly mistaken if we assume that the necessary skills will somehow take care of themselves.

How could we teach these skills, if we had a mind to do it? At Columbia University in the 1960s, David Caplovitz ran a graduate seminar at the old Bureau of Applied Social Research in which we simply read a number of research articles and monographs closely, as texts to be explicated. I recall among them *Union Democracy, The Academic Mind,* and a market research report called "They Changed to Tea." In each case we asked how the author went about telling the story (and that was the phrase we used). We read these materials almost line by line, asking why the author chose to present this table here, what question from the reader it anticipated, how the narrative flow could have been better managed. Along the way we learned some useful if now rather old-fashioned research methods; more important, we picked up the knack, indispensable for any good writer or editor, of putting ourselves in our readers' place, seeing our text through their eyes.

Only later did I realize how valuable—and how unusual—was the training I got, both in this course and through the examples of professors like Paul Lazarsfeld, Robert Merton, and the recently late C. Wright Mills: very different men, very different sociologists, but alike in their attention to the narrative side of their craft.

A story about Paul Lazarsfeld: A Viennese immigrant, he did not write "elegant" English, but by the time I knew him it was sturdy, workmanlike, and jargon-free. Perhaps because it was not his native language, he thought about how to write it, and he was not embarrassed to ask for help or to ask questions about it. Sometimes he even asked his research assistant. Once, when I used the word *interrelationship,* Lazarsfeld asked me what the difference was between that word and *relation.* I couldn't say. I still can't. "About three syllables, isn't it?" he suggested.

The Rhetoric of Sociology

Why would anyone say "interrelationship"? That leads us to another reason for stilted and cumbersome prose. Insofar as some of our kindred give any thought to expression at all, they want to sound "scientific"—not, as Mencken and Gowers suggest, from a desire to confuse the laity, but rather to impress their peers. A clotted, ponderous, stereotyped style is a rhetorical device, a badge meant to signal that one is an initiate, entitled to speak with authority. I will not belabor you with examples of the dismal effects, and I will come back to this matter of rhetoric. Right now I suggest only that this interpretation explains a great deal, from what one wag has called the "high colonic" style of article titles to the affectation of impersonality that leads to overuse of the passive voice.

On this last point: I have mentioned Wright Mills. His essay "On Intellectual Craftsmanship" appended to *The Sociological Imagination* needs to be updated for the personal computer age, but it is still one of the finest guides available to doing intellectual work. In it, Mills talks about the importance, first, of writing in one's own person with one's own voice; second, of writing with an audience in mind. In good Columbia University style, he works through the resulting fourfold table, concluding with the author who has no voice of his own and who speaks not to any audience but "solely for some record kept by no one." The result is "an autonomous sound in a great empty hall, all rather frightening, as in a Kafka novel, and it ought to be: we [are] talking about the edge of reason."

If this and other common defects of sociological writing come, as I am suggesting, from a desire to sound scientific, it indicates a disturbing lack of self-confidence. It also reflects a misunderstanding of what writing in the physical sciences can actually be like. True enough, the "hard" sciences are often hard to read, but most of the difficulty comes from their use of mathematics—mathematics used not just to show off, but because it is the most efficient way to express what is being expressed. When physical scientists can put their thoughts in plain English, often they really do. Consider their naming practices: what could be plainer than the language of "jumping genes," or "primordial soup," or "black holes"? Even when it comes to the ultimate beginning of everything, we find—a "big bang" (although Lewis Thomas has pointed out that a "great light" would actually be more accurate).

In physics, or biology, or chemistry, complicated ideas are sometimes expressed in the simplest of language—unpretentious, matter-of-fact, often even witty—bringing to mind Winston Churchill's dictum that "short words are best, and old words when short are best of all." If we must imitate the hard sciences, let us imitate that. Let us not seal the borders of our profession with an impenetrable style and vocabulary. Plainly, outsiders are not impressed.

In fact, it is not even clear that sociologese impresses the insiders it is meant to impress. I do not believe that Mills, Lazarsfeld, Merton, and other good writers in our discipline have suffered for their intelligibility (although, of course, they did have something of importance to say). On the other hand, some truly dreadful writers—and you can fill in the names yourself— have not received the ridicule and abuse that they deserve. I am not saying that they should have been ignored: occasionally they have actually had something to say that was worth the trouble. Nor am I suggesting that good writing be rewarded (aside from a little admiration, perhaps, when it is really good): the Southern Sociological Society does not need to offer a writing prize.

What I am saying is that competent writing, like sound methodology, should be expected. Its absence should be grounds for criticism. Until we begin to penalize bad writers, or at least to comment on their badness, we will get the prose we deserve. In seventeen years of editing book reviews for *Social Forces,* I cannot recall more than a half-dozen commenting that a book was poorly written. These were surely not the only ones. Either our reviewers cannot tell bad writing when they see it or (more likely) they think it inappropriate to criticize it. Either way, Q.E.D.

Why are we reluctant to take communication as seriously as theory or methodology? In part, I fear, it is because many of us regard good writing as mere ornament, if not as narcissistic and time-wasting. More than that: although we may not actually punish sociologists who are good writers, at some level we may not entirely trust them. I have been discussing communication as if the content itself were unproblematic, as if it were just a matter of clearing the verbal brush to make straight the path to meaning, but of course it is not that simple. People who are handy with words can use them not only to make their meanings clear but also to persuade—and scholars who have been trained to be persuaded only by evidence and deductive logic may feel, as Walter Prescott Webb put it, that "there is something naughty about good writing"; somehow it is better that truth be "made so ugly that nobody could doubt its virginity." In other words, we may actually tend to trust clumsy writers more: if they persuade us it is despite their ineptitude.

Scientific "Literature"

But here the ground has been cut from under our feet by the corrosive relativism of those literary theorists I mentioned earlier. The recognition that scientific discourse is just that, a mode of discourse, subject to the same kinds of analysis as poetry, political oratory, or comic books—that recognition can be exhilarating or profoundly dispiriting, but these days it can hardly be avoided. It is interesting that some other social science disciplines have begun to examine their "literatures" as literature, to take seriously how anthropological, and psychological, and economic narratives are constructed.

Clifford Geertz, for example, in a delightful little book called *Works and Lives,* writes of ethnography that "the pervasive questioning of standard modes of text-construction not only leaves easy realism less easy; it leaves it less persuasive." He observes that "the pretense of looking at the world directly, as though through a one-way screen . . . is itself a rhetorical strategy, a mode of persuasion; one it may well be difficult wholly to abandon and still be read, or wholly to maintain and still be believed." He points out that "the idea that reality has an idiom in which it prefers to be described" is a strange one, that in fact "the writing of ethnography involves telling stories, making pictures, concocting symbolisms, and deploying tropes."

Geertz proceeds to examine four distinguished anthropologists as literary stylists. He shows, for example, how E. E. Evans-Pritchard's strategy for building texts (Geertz calls it "Akobo Realism") is used to "demonstrate that nothing, no matter how singular, resists reasoned description." Likewise, he shows how Ruth Benedict's style, "at once spare, assured, lapidary, and above all resolute [with] definite views, definitely expressed" serves her purpose of "edificatory ethnography, anthropology designed to improve."

That is all very well, you may say, but these are anthropologists, half poets to begin with. Naturally their writing yields to this sort of treatment. And maybe it is no surprise when a psychologist like Jerome Bruner points to the importance of storytelling in his discipline: after all, psychology has its mushy aspects, too. Oddly enough, though, one of the most forthright discussions of the literary character of social science discourse has come from an economist, Donald McCloskey, who has taken it on himself to examine "how economists actually persuade each other, in print and in the hallways."

McCloskey concludes that what economists write has "much in common with poems and novels, that economists are story-tellers," that to understand how they work "it is useful to apply the methods of classical rhetoric." In an engaging discussion of why economists believe that demand varies inversely with price, for example, McCloskey estimates that "something on the order of fifteen percent" of the persuasion has come from "scientific" sources like modeling, empirical observation, and experimentation; the rest has come from such considerations as introspection, tradition, analogy, and individual authority. Even aesthetics play a part: "If there is a Law of Supply . . . it is hard to resist the charm of a Law of Demand to match." (I find it charming that an economist can come up with such a precise estimate. Fifteen percent, indeed.)

The point of such analysis, McCloskey believes, is that "the economist who understands his rhetoric is like the neurotic who has undergone psychoanalysis." In his view, understanding the rhetorical nature of scientific discourse is liberating.

To be sure, this approach can be taken to radical extremes that deny any inherent meaning in discourse at all. As Bruner observes, though, it takes a very expensive education at someplace like Duke University to bring most readers to that debilitating conclusion. I am just an old, country positivist myself and want to stop well short of that. But a conservative version of this tack is useful. It led, for example, to my observation that boring or obscure prose can be a rhetorical device used to claim authority. Viewed in this light, such writing becomes no more or less legitimate than any other "unscientific" method of persuasion. All need equally to be analyzed and, if necessary, discounted.

It follows that we are free to be good writers, in the conventional sense: to express ourselves clearly, to be interesting, even entertaining. We are free not only to enjoy what we do but to be seen to enjoy it. We are free to package the scientific contents of our work however we wish, and there is nothing wrong with an attractive package.

Sociology in the Marketplace

Moreover, if you accept the proposition that there really are some contents there, some packages display them better than others. And, to extend the metaphor, an attractive package that displays the contents to advantage can create new markets for the product. If others are not interested in what sociologists have to say, it is partly because they cannot understand us without inordinate difficulty. If we find some of our colleagues to be awkward or obscure writers, how much patience can we expect from the reading public? Even when they make the effort to understand us, though, outsiders conclude far too often that it is not worth it. And this leads to my second major point, which is that much of what we have to say is of no interest to them. A cynic would say that much of it is of no interest to anybody; I would say just that much is interesting only to those with graduate training in sociology.

I do not want to overstate our uselessness. Certainly our influence on other academic disciplines has been considerable, if not always appreciated (in either sense of that word). Our research methods, in particular, have found wide and often remunerative application in what is sometimes styled the "real world." Powerful explanatory theory, if we ever achieve it, will undoubtedly be of great interest to many people. But meanwhile most of what we do seems to have little to say to the "general reader," the occasional best-seller notwithstanding.

This is a new development. I challenge you to pick up an issue of *Social Forces* or the *American Sociological Review* from thirty-odd years ago and compare it to a recent issue. Just read the tables of contents and ask yourself whether a moderately intelligent and curious college graduate might want to read any of the articles. Things have changed.

Opinions will differ about whether this is regrettable. Some would say, I am sure, that it is a natural and inevitable result of sociology's maturation, that professional scientists necessarily write for each other and what scientists find interesting are questions generated by the internal dynamics of their discipline. That is a rather naive view of science, but there is some truth in it, and I am certainly not suggesting that all of us should choose our problems or write our books and articles with a nonsociological audience in mind.

Still, if the radicals of the 1960s did nothing else worthwhile, they reraised the question, "Sociology for what?" Disciplinary solipsism is probably unhealthy, and it is certainly short-sighted. If our fellow citizens find sociology useless and boring—well, we have no inherent right to their support.

So what do we do that the public appreciates? To answer that, let me suggest that there are two kinds of sociology: call them "ideal types" if you think I am oversimplifying. On one hand is the sort of hypothesis-testing and theory-building that we hold in highest esteem— rewarding it, for example, with publication in our major journals. On the other is work that applies the concepts and methods of our discipline to the understanding of particular societies, particular groups, particular institutions. In general, this narrative or interpretive sociology is less highly valued than the other, less highly valued than it once was, and (I would argue) less highly valued than it should be, if for no other reason than because it is the kind of sociology non-sociologists most often find worthwhile. Most of them would agree with Immanuel Wallerstein's assertion that "the purpose of abstractions is to arrive at specificity," not the other way around. In other words, they like it when we tell them sociologically informed stories: about themselves, about other men and women in their society, about other times and places.

Let me give you an example. Not long ago I taught an undergraduate course on the South in the 1920s and 1930s. Two of the books we read were *Human Factors in Cotton Culture* (1929) by Rupert Vance, and *A Preface to Peasantry* (1936) by Arthur Raper. It is a marvelous fact that both of those books were doctoral dissertations in sociology at the University of North Carolina. I mean no disrespect for our recent Ph.D.s when I venture to doubt that many of their dissertations will be worth reading after fifty years. But those two books surely are, although and maybe even because they probably would not be accepted as dissertations today. They could be called "merely descriptive," but they are powerful, detailed, authoritative, and (I might add) well written. They verge on "thick description" from two decades before Clifford Geertz coined that phrase and urged us to do it. These works employ what Jerome Bruner calls the "bottom-up" approach to inquiry, which he compares to "top-down," hypothesis-testing science. He argues that neither should be treated as a second-class citizen in the republic of intellect, and I want to do the same for our little corner of that republic.

Top-down science you understand. It is the model that most sociologists are taught to aspire to. It is, demonstrably, a powerful way to work. Aided by the "prosthetic devices" of logic, mathematics, and computers, as Bruner puts it, it can lead to "good theory, tight analysis, logical proof, sound argument, and empirical discovery guided by reasoned hypothesis." But this approach has its shortcomings. One of them is that it tends to produce insensitivity to the context within which inquiry is being conducted, unrealistically abstracting results from time and place.

The bottom-up approach does not have that problem; if anything, it can be too concerned with context, too particularistic (to use a good Parsonsianism). If its practitioners are literary scholars, they explore the world of a literary work; if they are economists, they may look at the structure of an industry or market; if they are sociologists they may take us inside a delinquent gang or a convent, a social movement, an ethnic group, or a Georgia county, and show us how it operates. This kind of work does not lead to theoretical statements of the form "Given conditions A, B, and C, X will produce Y." It may lead to modest generalizations of the form "Under certain circumstances, people are likely to do X," but even that is not the point. The point is to understand the particular case in hand.

As I said, the two approaches are ideal types, and some works combine them more or less successfully. At lunch one day, some of us were discussing Berton Kaplan's book, *Blue Ridge,* a study done in

Celo, North Carolina, of the stress brought on by modernization. When a late arrival asked what we were talking about, I said a study of Celo; simultaneously, another man said a study of stress. I had read the book as a story about a North Carolina mountain town; my colleague had read it as a test of an hypothesis. I guess we were both right.

But Bruner observes that these two styles of work correspond to different modes of thought. He quotes William James: "To say that all human thinking is essentially of two kinds—reasoning on the one hand, and narrative, descriptive, contemplative thinking on the other—is to say only what every reader's experience will corroborate." I like the combination, but only the rare scholar is adept at both, and it may be especially difficult to combine them in a single piece of work.

In any case, we do have a division of labor in sociology. Many of our community studies are essentially descriptive in this sense. So are many ethnographies, much of our historical sociology, and even many reports of survey research. But our division of labor is one in which the idiographers are too often regarded as hewers of wood and drawers of water for the nomothetes. Often they respond like members of other subordinate castes by trying to "pass," in this case, as practitioners of hypothetico-deductive science.

I would argue that they should be unashamedly what they are. Geertz describes Evans-Pritchard's view of anthropology's task as "the informing of informed opinion . . . in the matter of primitives, as others inform it about Homer, Italian painting, or the English civil war." Surely we can find an honorable place in our discipline for work that is simply informative, work that does not pretend to be about theory-building.

This way of doing sociology is not mere pandering, throwing scraps to the public to keep them paying our salaries. Nor is it second-rate intellectual activity—what you do if you don't have the right stuff for real Science. Instead, it is a different but equally respectable approach to our subject matter, a different but equally respectable use for our conceptual and methodological apparatus. To paraphrase the eminent Tudor historian G. R. Elton, a good many people just want to know about society for their own emotional or intellectual satisfaction, and we serve a useful social function when we help them to know better by description and interpretation. This does not make us merely entertainers; rather, it gives us a cultural role, as contributors to the nonpractical activities that make up our society's culture. A scholar who stimulates and satisfies the imagination, Elton observes, does not differ essentially from the poet or artist, and there is satisfaction of a high order in extending the "comprehending intelligence."

For what it is worth, narrative and kindred approaches to sociological work may now have intellectual fashion on their side. In the 1980s historians, prodded by Lawrence Stone and others, began to wonder aloud if they had been too quick to despise narrative history. Among literary critics there has been a vogue for something called the "new historicism," which seems often to degenerate into Marxism of a distressingly vulgar sort but at least attempts to treat literature in its social context. In the social sciences as well, what Bruner calls "the voices of the left hand" have been heard more loudly since the 1970s; as Geertz puts it, many have turned "away from a laws and instances ideal of explanation toward a cases and interpretation one."

These developments in our sister disciplines have had at least faint echoes in ours, and I suggest that, for us, they represent something of a revival of older ways—the way of Rupert Vance and Arthur Raper in those splendid books I mentioned; the way also of Guy Johnson, and Charles Johnson, and Harriet Herring, and Edgar Thompson, and of Howard Odum in his less "theoretical" works. Robert Coles observed once of the Southern sociologists of the 1930s that even the titles of their books "suggest, in their directness and simplicity, what disciplines like sociology and psychology have lost in recent years." Those books, he says, were "meant to alert the reader, keep his attention, and (in the Southern tradition) describe. Narrative power is what those books have." They were intellectual craftsmanship of a high order, but as much literary as scientific.

Moreover, as Coles has written elsewhere, the authors of those books were "scholars unafraid to demonstrate in clear, literate prose both compassion and a capacity to tolerate and describe life's complexities without reducing them to the simplifications of ideological rhetoric." Gunnar Myrdal made a similar point: he remarked approvingly in *An American Dilemma* that Southern social scientists were not as "purely scientific" as their Northern colleagues because they were unscientifically concerned with "human happiness"; an unscientific "statesmanship," he said, kept creeping into their writings. As Bruner observes, where science leads to results that are merely conclusive or inconclusive, narrative can be absurd, or sad, or comic. Narrative can call for a response beyond simple acknowledgment—for laughter, for pity, for anger. The great Southern sociologists of the 1930s were not afraid to reach for such responses.

Perhaps I should not overemphasize the Southern connection here. There is no distinctive "Southern sociology," and there should not be. To be sure, some of us believe that particularism pervades Southern culture, and if we are even halfway right about that, Southerners may tend to do sociology somewhat differently: to tell stories about Celo, for instance, rather than testing hypotheses about stress. But all of my points could be illustrated with examples from other places. Most Southern sociologists practice the nationally advertised brands of sociology, and rightly so. We are inextricably part of a national—indeed, international—enterprise.

But there is plainly a market for the sort of descriptive sociology at which the regionalists excelled. If sociologists disdain it, someone else will do it, and I would like to believe they cannot do it as well. To the extent that we have gotten out of this line of work, I think we have lost something valuable. And if it is a worthy job for sociologists—well, no one is better equipped for the narrative task than sociologists from our region. We are, after all, heirs to great storytelling traditions.

Bibliography

Acton, John Emerich Edward Dalberg. *The History of Freedom and Other Essays.* Edited by J. N. Figgis and R. V. Laurence. London: Macmillan and Company, 1922.

Agar, Herbert, and Allen Tate, eds. *Who Owns America? A New Declaration of Independence.* Boston: Houghton Mifflin, 1936.

Berelson, Bernard, and Gary A. Steiner. *Human Behavior: An Inventory of Scientific Findings.* New York: Harcourt, Brace, and World, 1964.

Black, Earl, and Merle Black. *Politics and Society in the South.* Cambridge: Harvard University Press, 1987.

Black, Merle. "The Modification of a Major Cultural Belief: Declining Support for 'Strict Segregation' among White Southerners, 1961–1972." *Journal of the North Carolina Political Science Association* 1 (Summer 1979): 4–21.

Brazil, Wayne. *Howard W. Odum: The Building Years, 1884–1930.* New York: Garland, 1988.

Britt, Steuart Henderson. *The Social Psychology of Modern Life.* New York: Holt Rinehart, 1941.

Brown, Richard Maxwell. "Southern Violence vs. the Civil Rights Movement, 1954–1968." In Vol. 1 of *Perspectives on the American South: An Annual Review of Society, Politics and Culture,* edited by Merle Black and J. S. Reed. New York: Gordon and Breach Science Publishers, 1981.

Brown, Roger. "Mass Phenomena." In *Handbook of Social Psychology,* edited by Gardner Lindzey. Reading, Mass.: Addison-Wesley, 1954.

Bruner, Jerome. *Actual Minds, Possible Worlds.* Cambridge: Harvard University Press, 1986.

Cantril, Hadley. *The Psychology of Social Movements.* Huntington, N.Y.: R. E. Krieger, 1941.

Carmichael, Peter A. "Jeeter Lester, Agrarian Par Excellence." *Sewanee Review* 48 (1940): 21–29.

Cash, W. J. *The Mind of the South.* New York: Alfred A. Knopf, 1941.

Chafe, William. *Civilities and Civil Rights.* New York: Oxford University Press, 1980.

Coles, Robert. *Farewell to the South.* Boston: Little, Brown, 1963.

———. *Migrants, Sharecroppers, Mountaineers.* Boston: Little, Brown, 1967.

Couch, W. T. "An Agrarian Programme for the South." *American Review* 3 (1934): 313–26.

———. "The Agrarian Romance." *South Atlantic Quarterly* 36 (1937): 419–30.

Cram, Ralph Adams. *Convictions and Controversies.* Boston: Marshall Jones Company, [1935].

Davidson, Chandler. *Biracial Politics: Conflict and Coalition in the Metropolitan South.* Baton Rouge: Louisiana State University Press, 1972.

Davidson, Donald. *The Attack on Leviathan: Regionalism and Nationalism in the United States.* Chapel Hill: University of North Carolina Press, 1938.

———. "Regionalism as Social Science." *Southern Review* o.s. 3 (1937): 209–24.

———. "A Sociologist in Eden." *American Review* 8 (1936): 177–204.

———. "Where Regionalism and Sectionalism Meet." *Social Forces* 13 (1934): 23–31.

———. "Why the Modern South Has a Great Literature." In Vol. 1 of *Vanderbilt Studies in the Humanities,* edited by Richmond C. Beatty, J. Philip Hyatt, and Monroe K. Spears. Nashville: Vanderbilt University Press, 1951.

Dollard, John, et al. *Frustration and Aggression.* New Haven: Yale University Press, 1939.

Doyle, Bertram W. *The Etiquette of Race Relations in the South: A Study in Social Control.* Chicago: University of Chicago Press, [1937].

Edel, Candace Kim, et al. "Uneven Regional Development: An Introduction to This Issue." *Review of Radical Political Economics* 10.3 (Fall 1978): 1–12.

Elton, G. R. *The Practice of History.* New York: Thomas Y. Crowell, 1967.

Erikson, Kai. "On Writing Social Science." *Social Science* 72 (1987): 97–102.

Gallup Report, no. 185 (February 1981).

Gans, Herbert. *The Urban Villagers: Group and Class in the Life of Italian-Americans.* New York: Free Press of Glencoe, 1962.

Geertz, Clifford. *The Interpretation of Cultures.* New York: Basic Books, 1973.
———. *Local Knowledge: Further Essays in Interpretive Anthropology.* New York: Basic Books, 1983.
———. *Works and Lives: The Anthropologist as Author.* Stanford, Calif.: Stanford University Press, 1988.
Gilbert, G. M. "Stereotype Persistence and Change among College Students." *Journal of Abnormal and Social Psychology* 46 (1951): 245–54.
Gowers, Sir Ernest. *The Complete Plain Words.* Boston: David R. Godine, 1988.
Greeley, Andrew M. *Building Coalitions.* New York: New Viewpoints, 1974.
Greeley, Andrew M., and Paul B. Sheatsley, "Attitudes toward Racial Integration." *Scientific American* (December 1971): 13–19.
Hackney, Sheldon. "Southern Violence." *American Historical Review* 74 (1969): 906–25.
Hayes, Carlton J. H. *Essays on Nationalism.* New York: Russell and Russell, 1966.
Hobson, Fred C., Jr. *Serpent in Eden: H. L. Mencken and the South.* Chapel Hill: University of North Carolina Press, 1974.
Hoepfner, Theodore. "Economics of Agrarianism." *Mississippi Quarterly* 13 (1960): 61–68.
Hovland, Carl Iver, and Robert R. Sears. "Minor Studies of Aggression: VI. Correlation of Lynchings with Economic Indices," *Journal of Psychology* 9 (1940): 301–10.
Hyman, Herbert H., and Paul B. Sheatsley, "Attitudes toward Desegregation." *Scientific American* (July 1964): 16–23.
Jacoby, Russell. *The Last Intellectuals: American Culture in the Age of Academe.* New York: Basic Books, 1987.
Johnson, Guy Benton, and Guion Griffis Johnson. *Research in Service to Society: The First Fifty Years of the Institute for Research in Social Science at the University of North Carolina.* Chapel Hill: University of North Carolina Press, 1980.
Kaplan, Berton H. *Blue Ridge: An Appalachian Community in Transition.* Morgantown: Appalachian Center, West Virginia University, 1971.
Karlins, Marvin, Thomas L. Coffman, and Gary Walters. "On the Fading of Social Stereotypes: Studies in Three Generations of College Students." *Journal of Personality and Social Psychology* 13 (1969): 1–16.
Katz, Daniel, and Kenneth Braley. "Racial Stereotypes of One Hundred College Students." *Journal of Abnormal and Social Psychology* 28 (1933): 280–90.

Kedourie, Elie. *Nationalism*. London: Hutchinson and Co., 1960.

Kirby, Jack Temple. *Rural Worlds Lost: The American South, 1920–1960*. Baton Rouge: Louisiana State University Press, 1987.

Laqueur, Walter. "The Hitler-Stalin Coalition." *Wall Street Journal* (November 25, 1988): 9.

Lowrey, Burling. "Sports 'Sociologese.'" *Virginia Quarterly Review* 63 (1987): 532–38.

McCloskey, Donald N. *The Rhetoric of Economics*. Madison: University of Wisconsin Press, 1985.

———. "The Rhetoric of Economics." *Social Science* 71 (1986): 97–102.

Markusen, Ann R. *Regions: The Economics and Politics of Territory*. Totowa, N.J.: Rowan and Littlefield, 1987.

Matthews, Donald R., and James W. Prothro. *Negroes and the New Southern Politics*. New York: Harcourt, Brace, and World, 1966.

Matthews, Ralph. *The Creation of Regional Dependency*. Toronto: University of Toronto Press, 1983.

Mencken, H. L. "Professor Veblen." In *Prejudices: First Series*. New York: Alfred A. Knopf, 1919.

———. "The Sahara of the Bozart." In *American Essays,* edited by Charles B. Shaw. New York: Pelican Mentor Books, 1948.

Mills, C. Wright. *The Sociological Imagination*. New York: Oxford University Press, 1959.

Mims, Edwin. *The Advancing South: Stories of Progress and Reaction*. Garden City, N.Y.: Doubleday, Page & Company, 1926.

Mintz, Alexander. "A Re-examination of Correlations between Lynchings and Economic Indicators." *Journal of Abnormal and Social Psychology* 41 (April 1946): 154–60.

Morison, Samuel Eliot. "History as a Literary Art." (1946). In *Sailor Historian: The Best of Samuel Eliot Morison*. Boston: Houghton Mifflin, 1977.

Murray, Albert. *South to a Very Old Place*. New York: McGraw-Hill, 1971.

Myrdal, Gunnar. *An American Dilemma: The Negro Problem and Modern Democracy*. New York: Harper and Brothers, 1944.

Newby, Idus A. "The Southern Agrarians: A View after Thirty Years." *Agricultural History* 37 (1963): 143–55.

Nock, Albert Jay. "Thoughts from Abroad." In *Free Speech and Plain Language*. New York: William Morrow and Company, 1937.

O'Brien, Michael. *The Idea of the American South, 1920–1941*. Baltimore: Johns Hopkins University Press, 1979.

Odum, Howard W. *An American Epoch: Southern Portraiture in the National Picture.* New York: Henry Holt, 1930.

——. *Cold Blue Moon: Ulysses Afar Off.* Indianapolis: Bobbs-Merrill, 1931.

——. *Folk, Region, and Society: Selected Papers of Howard W. Odum.* Edited by Katherine Jocher et al. Chapel Hill: University of North Carolina Press, 1964.

——. *Race and Rumors of Race.* Chapel Hill: University of North Carolina Press, 1943.

——. *Rainbow Round My Shoulder: The Blue Trail of Black Ulysses.* Indianapolis: Bobbs-Merrill, 1928.

——. *Southern Regions of the United States.* Chapel Hill: University of North Carolina Press, 1936.

——. *The Way of the South.* New York: Macmillan, 1947.

——. *Wings on My Feet: Black Ulysses at the Wars.* Indianapolis: Bobbs-Merrill, 1929.

Orwell, George. *The Lion and the Unicorn: Socialism and the English Genius.* London: Secker and Warburg, 1962.

Owsley, Frank L. "The Pillars of Agrarianism." *American Review* 4 (1935): 529–47.

Pettigrew, Thomas F. "Regional Differences in Anti-Negro Prejudice." In *Racial Attitudes in America,* edited by John C. Brigham and Theodore A. Weissbach. New York: Harper and Row, 1972.

Phillips, Ulrich B. "The Central Theme of Southern History." *American Historical Review* 34 (October 1928): 31.

Pressly, Thomas J. "Agrarianism: An Autopsy." *Sewanee Review* 49 (1941): 145–63.

Purdy, Rob Roy, ed. *Fugitives' Reunion: Conversations at Vanderbilt, May 3–5, 1956.* Nashville: Vanderbilt University Press, 1959.

Ransom, John Crowe. *God without Thunder: An Unorthodox Defense of Orthodoxy.* New York: Harcourt, Brace, and Company [1930].

——. "Happy Farmers." *American Review* 1 (1933): 513–35.

——, et al. "A Symposium: The Agrarians Today," *Shenandoah* 3 (Summer 1952): 14–33.

Raper, Arthur F. *Preface to Peasantry: A Tale of Two Black Belt Counties.* Chapel Hill: University of North Carolina Press, 1936.

——. *The Tragedy of Lynching.* Chapel Hill: University of North Carolina Press, 1933.

Reed, John Shelton. "A Note on the Control of Lynching." *Public Opinion Quarterly* 33 (Summer 1969): 268–71.

———. *The Enduring South: Subcultural Persistence in Mass Society.* Rev. ed. Chapel Hill: University of North Carolina Press, 1986.

———. *One South: An Ethnic Approach to Regional Culture.* Baton Rouge: Louisiana State University Press, 1982.

———. "Reply to Tufte," *Public Opinion Quarterly* 33 (Winter 1969–1970): 625–26.

———. *Southerners: The Social Psychology of Sectionalism.* Chapel Hill: University of North Carolina Press, 1983.

Reed, Roy. "Revisiting the Southern Mind." *New York Times Magazine* (December 5, 1976): 42–43, 99–109.

Renan, Ernest. "Qu'est-ce qu-une nation?" In *Discours et Conférences.* Paris: Calmann-Lévy, 1887.

Rubin, Louis D. "Introduction to the Torchbook Edition." In *I'll Take My Stand: The South and the Agrarian Tradition.* New York: Harper Torchbooks, 1962.

———. *The Wary Fugitives: Four Poets and the South.* Baton Rouge: Louisiana State University Press [1978].

Schneider, Joseph E. "Support for New Christian Right Ideology among Fundamentalist Ministers in North Carolina." Paper presented to Southern Sociological Society Annual Meeting, Charlotte, N.C., 1985.

Schwartz, Mildred A. *Trends in White Attitudes toward Black People.* Chicago: National Opinion Research Center, 1967.

Sheatsley, Paul B. "White Attitudes toward the Negro." In *The Negro American,* edited by Talcott Parsons and Kenneth B. Clark. Boston: Beacon Press, 1967.

Shortridge, James R. "Changing Usage of Four American Regional Labels." *Annals of the Association of American Geographers* 77 (1987): 325–36.

Singal, Daniel Joseph. *The War Within: From Victorian to Modernist Thought in the South, 1919–1945.* Chapel Hill: University of North Carolina Press, 1982.

Smith, Anthony D. *The Ethnic Origins of Nationalism.* New York: Basil Blackwell, 1986.

———. *Theories of Nationalism.* London: Duckworth, 1971.

Smith, Henry. "The Dilemma of Agrarianism." *Southwest Review* 19 (1934): 215–32.

Sosna, Morton. *In Search of the Silent South: Southern Liberals and the Race Issue.* New York: Columbia University Press, 1977.

Southern, David W. *Gunnar Myrdal and Black-White Relations: The Use and Abuse of "An American Dilemma," 1944–1969.* Baton Rouge: Louisiana State University Press, 1987.

Stewart, Randall. "The Relation between Fugitives and Agrarians." *Mississippi Quarterly* 13 (1960): 55–60.

Stone, Lawrence. "The Revival of Narrative: Reflections on a New Old History." In *The Past and the Present.* Boston: Routledge and Kegan Paul, 1981.

Thomas, Lewis. *Late Night Thoughts on Listening to Mahler's Ninth Symphony.* New York: Viking Press, 1983.

Thompson, Edgar T. *Plantation Societies, Race Relations, and the South: The Regimentation of Populations. Selected Papers of Edgar T. Thompson.* Durham: Duke University Press, 1975.

Tindall, George B. "History and the English Language." *Perspectives* 22 (October 1984): 7–11.

———. "Howard W. Odum: A Preliminary Estimate" (1958). In *The Ethnic Southerners.* Baton Rouge: Louisiana State University Press, 1976.

Tuchman, Barbara. *Practicing History: Selected Essays.* New York: Alfred A. Knopf, 1981.

Tufte, Edward R. "A Note of Caution in Using Variables That Have Common Elements." *Public Opinion Quarterly* 33 (Winter 1969–1970): 622–24.

Twelve Southerners. *I'll Take My Stand: The South and the Agrarian Tradition.* New York: Harper and Brothers, 1930.

Vance, Rupert B. *All These People: The Nation's Human Resources in the South.* Chapel Hill: University of North Carolina Press, 1945.

———. "Howard Odum's Technicways: A Neglected Lead in American Sociology." *Social Forces* 50 (1972): 456–61.

———. *Human Factors in Cotton Culture: A Study in the Social Geography of the American South.* Chapel Hill: University of North Carolina Press, 1929.

———. *Human Geography of the South: A Study in Regional Resources and Human Adequacy.* Chapel Hill: University of North Carolina Press, 1935.

———. *Regionalism and the South: Selected Papers of Rupert Vance,* edited by John Shelton Reed and Daniel Joseph Singal. Chapel Hill: University of North Carolina Press, 1982.

———. *Research Memorandum on Population Redistribution within the United States.* New York: Social Science Research Council, 1938.

Vance, Rupert B., and Nicholas J. Demerath, eds. *The Urban South.* Chapel Hill: University of North Carolina Press, 1954.

Vance, Rupert B., John E. Ivey, Jr., and Marjorie N. Bond. *Exploring the South.* New York: Harcourt, Brace, and Company, 1949.

Wallerstein, Immanuel. "Some Reflections on History, the Social Sciences, and Politics." In *The Capitalist World-Economy.* New York: Cambridge University Press, 1979.

Weaver, Richard. "Agrarianism in Exile." *Sewanee Review* 58 (1950): 586–606.

Westie, Frank R. "Academic Expectations for Professional Immortality: A Study of Legitimation." *American Sociologist* 8 (1973): 19–32.

Woodward, C. Vann. *The Burden of Southern History.* Rev. ed. Baton Rouge: Louisiana State University Press, 1968.

———. "W. J. Cash Reconsidered." *New York Review of Books* 13 (December 4, 1969): 28–34.

Work, Monroe N. *Negro Yearbook, 1931–1932.* Tuskegee Institute, Ala.: Negro Yearbook Publishing Company, 1931.

Zelinsky, Wilbur. "North America's Vernacular Regions." *Annals of the Association of American Geographers* 70 (1980): 1–16.

Index